FIX FREEZE FEAST

THE DELICIOUS, MONEY-SAVING WAY TO FEED YOUR FAMILY

SECOND EDITION

KATI NEVILLE AND LINDSAY AHRENS

 Storey Publishing

The mission of Storey Publishing is to serve our customers by publishing practical information that encourages personal independence in harmony with the environment.

Edited by Deanna F. Cook and Sarah Guare
Art direction and book design by Jeff Stiefel
Text production by Jennifer Jepson Smith
Indexed by Samantha Miller
Cover and interior photography by © Alexandra
    Grablewski, except pages iii, 3–5, and 11 by
    Mars Vilaubi
Food styling by Cyd McDowell

Storey Publishing
210 MASS MoCA Way
North Adams, MA 01247
storey.com

Printed in China by Toppan Leefung Printing Ltd.
10 9 8 7 6 5 4 3 2 1

LIBRARY OF CONGRESS
CATALOGING-IN-PUBLICATION DATA

Names: Neville, Kati, author. | Ahrens, Lindsay,
    author.
Title: Fix, freeze, feast : the delicious, money-
    saving way to feed your family / Kati Neville
    and Lindsay Ahrens.
Description: 2nd edition. | North Adams, MA :
    Storey Publishing, 2018.
    | Includes bibliographical references and
    index.
Identifiers: LCCN 2017046699 (print)
    | LCCN 2017047757 (ebook)
    | ISBN 9781612129297 (ebook)
    | ISBN 9781612129280 (pbk. : alk. paper)
Subjects: LCSH: Make-ahead cooking. | Ready
    meals. | LCGFT: Cookbooks.
Classification: LCC TX833.5 (ebook)
    | LCC TX833.5 .N48 2018 (print)
    | DDC 641.5/55—dc23
LC record available at https://lccn.loc
    .gov/2017046699

TO OUR **FAMILIES**

CONTENTS

CHICKEN MAIN DISHES   18

BEEF MAIN DISHES 72

PORK MAIN DISHES 108

BREAKFAST, SNACKS, AND SWEETS 210

THE BEAUTY OF **MAKE-AHEAD MEALS**

Even with all the recipe books, cooking classes, how-to manuals, and television programs devoted to the subject of meal preparation, many of us still find ourselves hungry and disorganized by the time the dinner hour rolls around. There is no end to the excellent resources available, but our busy lives get the better of us, and all our good intentions can come to naught. We want to feed our families healthful, economical meals that taste great and do not require hours of work. How can we accomplish this when time is short and the demands of work and family are ever increasing?

This cookbook shows you how to fix several meals at one time. No doubt you're used to preparing a recipe from start to finish and then presenting a hot meal to your family. But our method is different: We scale the recipe using large quantities and then divide it into multiple meals. The meals are prepared right up to the final cooking stage. You then package and freeze them, and all you have to do is thaw one and cook it for dinner!

The purpose of this book is to make feeding your family easier. Following are just a few of the benefits you will enjoy when you use our recipes.

- **ECONOMY:** Every time you eat from your freezer you save money, especially if it takes the place of frequently eating out.

- **TIME MANAGEMENT:** If you normally shop daily and cook one meal at a time, we estimate our method will save you an hour or more every day.

- **CONVENIENCE:** Things come up: There are evenings when everyone in the family is busy; late or unplanned meetings cut into cooking time; children's school friends or other unexpected company stops by; a friend is in need. It is wonderful to have a few meals on hand, for every day or just in case.

- **ADAPTABILITY:** If you watch what you eat — for whatever reason — make-ahead meals will help you stay on track.

- **VARIETY:** An interesting selection of freezer meals integrated with fresh meals and the occasional restaurant treat will prevent food boredom.

- **FUN:** Work through your recipes with a friend or two. Sharing stories and laughter makes the time seem less like work and more like play.

- **ACCOMPLISHMENT:** It's a wonderful feeling to have nourishing food in the freezer and an organized and efficient approach to daily dinners.

As former owners of meal-preparation businesses, we bring you our best of the best in this book. Yes, these recipes are straight from our stash — tried, tested, and true. Our past customers have made many of these recipes countless times and rave about the delicious results. We are passionate about what we do and uncompromising in our commitment to using fresh, from-scratch ingredients wherever possible. We give you only dishes that meet the same standard we use to feed our own families.

Whether you're a novice or an advanced cook, a bargain shopper or someone with money to spare, a time-starved or a leisurely from-scratch cook, you'll find plenty of wonderful recipes and tips here!

ABOUT OUR FIX AND FREEZE RECIPES

Our recipes are presented in a different way than in a conventional cookbook. We've designed and tested the recipes to yield large quantities that are divided into several meals. This way, you are maximizing your use of time and the economy of scale. Preparing food intended to be frozen is different from preparing and cooking a meal fresh. Some foods freeze better cooked, while others freeze better raw; some foods don't freeze well at all and are best added fresh at dinnertime. As such, some of our recipes are a hybrid of cooked and raw components. All our recipes have been tested and written for maximum quality at mealtime.

If you're new to make-ahead meals, we suggest you start with one or two recipes at first. Consider choosing a recipe for a simple marinade poured over meat — a quick and delicious way to acquaint yourself with our method. Tequila-Lime Chicken, Honey-Glazed Chicken Thighs, An's Pork Chops, and Basil-Balsamic Chops are simple meals for beginners. Or you may want to look for recipes that are similar to dinner dishes you currently prepare. It never hurts to go with the tried and true.

If you already "batch cook," belong to a dinner co-op, or practice other forms of advance meal preparation, our recipes will work nicely with your current practices. Even if you have experience, we still recommend you start off with a few different recipes and gradually increase the number you do at one time.

Many of the recipes in this book are for entrées, but don't miss the other gems! We have included an assortment of brunch items, side dishes, snacks, sweets, and sauces. We offer a selection of meatless recipes and even some homemade spice mixes sprinkled throughout the chapters. Fill your freezer with main dishes or the extras — either way, you'll enjoy all the benefits of make-ahead meals.

FEAST TONIGHT RECIPES

You will notice that several recipes in this book are labeled "Feast Tonight." These meals are intended to be eaten without being frozen first and are the offspring of a few of our favorite recipes. (And, of course, you can always save one freezer meal from any of our other recipes and cook it that same night for dinner.)

For example, Dave's Swamp Blues Barbecued Chicken is a typical recipe that yields three freezer meals. The Feast Tonight recipes that follow it show you how to take one of those freezer meals and prepare it for use in either of these two fresh recipes: Dave's Skillet Hash or Dave's Barbecued Chicken Pizza. Feast Tonight recipes are a great way to add more mealtime variety while extending the economy and convenience of our make-ahead meals.

Also, check out page 238 for a list of recipes that can go directly from the freezer to the oven, skillet, or slow cooker — no thawing required.

Buy in bulk and make multiple portions of one recipe.

2 **Divide food into meals & label,
then stack in the freezer.**

RECIPE
Farmers' Market Soup

DIRECTIONS

Soup can be cooked when frozen o_
Put soup into a slow cooker. Add _
on low for 6 to 8 hours or on hig_
Stovetop: Put soup into pot. Add
over medium heat until lentils and
tender, about 40 minutes. Add addit_
cooking if desired.

RECIPE
Farmers' Market Soup

USE BY
Nov. 2019

DIRECTIONS

Soup can be cooked when frozen or thawed. Slow cooker:
Put soup into a slow cooker. Add 2 cups water. Cook
on low for 6 to 8 hours or on high for 3 to 4 hours.
Stovetop: Put soup into pot. Add 2 cups water. Simmer
over medium heat until lentils and vegetables are
tender, about 40 minutes. Add additional water during
cooking if desired.

3 Thaw & cook one meal for dinner and enjoy!

Farmers' Market Soup,
page 139

PLANNING FOR SUCCESS

We've found that it helps to start with a plan, even if it's just a mental list of steps we'll take. Thinking through what we want to accomplish helps keep us organized and efficient. We have broken our method into some simple steps, though these are by no means mandatory. Have fun and experiment with what works best for you. We encourage you to adapt our recipes to fit your lifestyle.

SCALABLE RECIPES

We've found it's most convenient to scale each recipe to yield large quantities that can be packaged into smaller portions. Most of our recipes are written to feed a family of four, but they can easily be divided further and packaged into smaller meals, or frozen in larger quantities for bigger families or appetites.

STEP 1) MAKE YOUR SHOPPING LIST & GO SHOPPING

Make a shopping list of the ingredients used in each recipe you intend to prepare. We suggest recording every ingredient, even if you know you have it on hand. Once your list is complete, go through the kitchen and mark off the items you already have. Now you know exactly what to buy at the store, and you also have a complete list from which to work when you make your chosen recipes.

We find it helpful to divide shopping lists according to food type: meat, dairy, vegetables, seasonings, dry goods, canned goods, and so on. Being organized will help you move more efficiently through crowded aisles on weekends or online grocery product lists.

If you're buying the main ingredient for a recipe in bulk, try to begin with total weights close to the amount called for in the recipe, but don't worry if you're a bit over or under. The recipes are flexible enough to accommodate small differences.

You can find ingredients in various states of preparation to make things easier on the cook. You can buy shredded cheese instead of bricks of cheese, peeled garlic cloves instead of whole heads of garlic, and chopped onion instead of whole onions. Before you choose an item, you'll want to consider the quantity you need, the preparation time you'll save, and how much money you'll pay for the convenience. Choose what will work best for you and your budget without compromising quality.

COMMON INGREDIENTS

Some common ingredients are available in several forms. We have chosen to list them one way throughout the book. Following is a list of common items with our preferred form and possible substitutions.

CHICKEN OR BEEF BASE: There are several ways to buy base or bouillon; we prefer products without monosodium glutamate (MSG). Our recipes call for 1 teaspoon of base to equal 1 cup of reconstituted broth. Some brands of bouillon and base are more or less concentrated, so read labels carefully to determine the correct amount to use depending on the form you've selected.

GARLIC: We prefer the freshness and flavor of mincing fresh garlic cloves. Use a chopper, food processor, knife, or garlic press. Bottled minced garlic is an acceptable substitute and is easy to measure out in large quantities.

GINGER: Peel and chop fresh gingerroot before mincing it in a food processor or mini chopper. It's well worth the effort of using fresh ginger for the superior flavor it imparts to the recipes.

ONION: In our recipes, "onion" refers to fresh onion, peeled and chopped, or minced in a food processor or mini chopper. If the recipe requires any other form — dried onion flakes, for example — the recipe will so indicate. Our recipes call for fresh onion to be chopped, diced, or minced. Chop and dice onion with a knife or food processor. Chopped pieces are roughly double the size of diced. Mincing is best done in a food processor, as it cuts the onion very fine, just short of a purée.

BREADCRUMBS: Our recipes using breadcrumbs all call for dry breadcrumbs. If not otherwise specified, choose either seasoned or plain.

BLACK PEPPER: Unless otherwise indicated, use any form you like — cracked, crushed, or ground.

RED PEPPER FLAKES: In some stores, the container may say "crushed red pepper."

SCALLIONS: In some stores, scallions are called green onions.

VEGETABLE COOKING SPRAY: The cooking directions in each relevant recipe indicate whether a baking dish is greased or ungreased. Please note that "greased" does not necessarily refer to the use of butter or oil but can also mean using a vegetable cooking spray

PREP YOUR KITCHEN

A clean and tidy kitchen is helpful for organized and successful cooking. Before you begin, empty the sink and dishwasher, clear the countertops, and have a large, empty trash can handy. Set the nonperishables on the counter. It's more efficient to do this ahead rather than locating one thing at a time while you are cooking. If you're planning to prepare several recipes at once, try to have some space cleared in your freezer so you don't have to stop and shuffle things around to make room for your packages.

Keep in mind that when cooking recipes with large yields, the bowls, skillets, and pots need to be large enough to accommodate the ingredients.

The following is a list of items we suggest you have on hand:

- Extra measuring cups and spoons

- Large liquid measuring cup with a spout

- Large stainless steel bowls

- Very large stockpot (8-quart capacity or larger)

- Boxes, containers, or cans for holding your bags open and steady for easy filling (Refer to the packaging and freezing tips on pages 10 and 12.)

PREP YOUR INGREDIENTS

Our recipes list most ingredients in a "ready-to-go" state. This means the ingredient list includes brief instructions for readying the items to be added to the dish. In the Teriyaki Chicken recipe, for example, the phrase "skin removed" is in the ingredient list, directly after the chicken thigh listing. Further down, the recipe calls for minced garlic and minced ginger. These recipe-ready cues indicate that you should remove the skin and mince both the garlic and ginger before you begin making the recipe.

If you are making more than one recipe at a time, it can be helpful to make a list of preparation steps for each recipe on the back of the shopping list. One consolidated list helps to readily identify opportunities to combine tasks wherever possible. For instance, if two recipes call for chopped onion, combine the quantities and chop enough onion for both recipes at once. Having one sheet of paper with both shopping and prep lists is also convenient. It's available for quick reference out at the store and then again back in the kitchen.

You're almost ready to begin with the first recipe you selected. We recommend you also create labels for the food you will be preparing. After completing your preparation tasks, get out the number of freezer containers you'll need and label them before moving through each recipe. It's much easier to label flat bags than filled ones. Labels for baking dishes can be affixed to or written directly on the wrap. Labeling your meals is the only way to avoid "freezer surprise" — frozen food without a name or date to indicate how long it has been in there. There are different labeling options available to you; some are listed below.

- If you know you'll be keeping all the meals for yourself, use a permanent marker to write the date, recipe name, and page number on the bag. This allows you to refer to the book for the cooking instructions.

- Go to www.storey.com/freezer-labels and print PDFs of the labels on large Avery stickers. The online templates work with Avery labels (types 5265, 5165, 8165, 8665, 8465, 8255), available wherever office supplies are sold.

BEST CONTAINERS FOR FREEZING

We suggest using packaging designed specifically for freezer use. Home cooks will sometimes try to reuse packaging like cottage cheese or yogurt containers, for example, but those will not protect food as well as containers tested for freezing temperatures. Our favorite packaging for freezing includes the following:

- Zip-top freezer bags in several sizes, especially 1-gallon and 1-quart
- Freezable plastic containers, 8-cup (64-ounce) size
- Aluminum pans
- Aluminum foil
- Parchment paper
- Plastic wrap
- Tempered glass pans and other bakeware
- Tempered glass jars, such as those suitable for canning

We always try to avoid waste, so we will wash and reuse foil pans when we can. Freezable round containers in the 64-ounce size are perfect for soups and stews — pop frozen food out and place it directly in the slow cooker or pressure cooker.

STEP 5 | PREPARE YOUR MEALS

Now it's time to put it all together! In preparing our recipes, we encourage you to experiment. If you want to use less liquor than what's called for, do so. Add more garlic. Use more vegetables. Try to incorporate some of your family's preferences into your preparation. While you do so, make notes so you can remember what you did in order to duplicate your successes.

In all likelihood you are already practicing good food safety — washing your hands frequently, keeping raw meat separate from vegetables and condiments, and cleaning up spills promptly. Use hot, soapy water to clean equipment and cooking surfaces. Keep cold foods in the refrigerator or a cooler with ice until you're ready to use them in the recipe. Cook your foods to the appropriate temperatures, and be sure to never pour a hot sauce over raw meat.

To avoid food-borne illness, keep hot food above 140°F (60°C) and cold food below 40°F (4°C). Anywhere in between is considered a danger zone, conducive to bacterial growth. You will need to cool all hot sauces before they can be added to raw meats. To be safe, do this as quickly as possible.

When a recipe indicates you should cool a sauce, this is the proper way to do it: Pour the hot sauce into a large shallow pan. Use more than one pan if necessary, as the sauce should not be more than 4 inches deep. Leave the pan uncovered. Place the pan in the sink and carefully fill the sink with cold water and ice until the water reaches the outside rim of the pan. Stir the sauce in the pan frequently. When the sauce reaches 70°F (21°C), you can transfer it to the refrigerator to keep it cool until it's used in the recipe.

STEP 6 | FREEZE

Unless a power outage or some other event has compromised food safety, you can freeze food as long as you like. The food's texture and taste may suffer over the long term, but it will be safe to eat indefinitely. On each recipe, we have recommended freezer times for optimal results, though you needn't worry if you don't get to a particular entrée within the specified time frame — it will still be safe to consume.

TAKE EXTRA CARE WHEN WORKING WITH GLASS. Choose pans marked freezer-safe. To select jars, look for a wide-mouth style suitable for canning. Leave 2 inches of headspace when filling the jars and chill food in the refrigerator before freezing with the lids off. Once frozen, gently secure the lids. Handle frozen glass carefully and avoid sudden temperature changes; it's best to thaw a meal in a glass pan before baking.

If you have a vacuum sealer, feel free to use it on your freezer meals but don't go to the expense just for this use — it will extend the length of time you can freeze your food without loss of quality, but we find we eat the meals well within the normal time frame specified in the recipe. Our recommended freezing times are based on the packaging we recommend using in each recipe. Wrap food tightly in packaging and remove as much air as you can. Carefully packaging and freezing your freezer meals will ensure the best quality when dinnertime comes around.

BEST AND WORST CANDIDATES FOR FREEZING

When it comes to ingredients that do and do not freeze well, we've done years of testing.

- **FRESH FOODS WITH A HIGH WATER CONTENT,** such as lettuces and cucumbers, do not freeze well at all. Others, like cabbage, kale, celery, and leafy herbs, freeze fine with the right treatment — either par-cooked or raw in a sauce or a soup.

- **DAIRY PRODUCTS,** such as milk, cream, sour cream, cottage cheese, and half-and-half, do not freeze well on their own. However, we find they do well in our recipes, especially when full-fat dairy is used. Dairy-based sauces may separate but will come back together with gentle mixing after thawing and heating.

- **CHEESE** freezes best when shredded.

- **COOKED RICE AND PASTA** freeze best when they are prepared until just done or slightly underdone. Good packaging practices are important because these ingredients can easily take on off-flavors.

- **FRIED FOODS** do not freeze well; they become soggy.

- **RAW POTATO** does not freeze well. Cook it first to keep it from turning black.

THAW, COOK, AND ENJOY!

We specify in every recipe that you should completely thaw your frozen items in the refrigerator — not on the counter and never in hot water. Correctly thawing meat and cooking it to appropriate temperatures are the best way to avoid foodborne illness. We have found, however, that many of our recipes can go successfully from the freezer to the oven, grill, or slow cooker. For a list of the recipes that you can confidently cook from frozen, see page 238.

Cook all meat to the temperature indicated in the directions. The temperature of some meats will continue to rise after you remove the meat from the oven or grill, so you may remove the meat from the heat source when it is a few degrees below the indicated temperature as long as you are sure it will reach the required temperature before it is eaten.

Once an entrée has been thawed, you must cook it. Never thaw raw meat and then refreeze it.

As for the cooking methods, we have listed what we find works best for each recipe. It's up to you if you want to alter the method. You may choose to bake a dish for which the recipe calls for grilling, or use the slow cooker instead of the oven. In many cases, an alternative cooking method will work well.

Once you enjoy make-ahead meals a time or two, you will quickly realize how much time, energy, and money you save cooking this way!

WHAT IS THE BEST WAY TO . . .

MAKE THE MOST OF MY LIMITED FREEZER SPACE?
This method will work even for cooks with limited freezer space. You may be surprised at how much food can fit in a standard freezer. Following are tips for conserving freezer space:

- Choose recipes for dishes that will be stored in plastic freezer bags rather than in baking dishes. Freeze these meals flat; once frozen, line them up vertically (as you would books on a shelf).

- Make only one or two recipes at a time.

- Pick recipes with lower yields. Stick to those recipes that make two or three freezer meals each rather than those that yield larger numbers.

- Consider trading freezer meals with a friend to maximize variety while conserving freezer space (see our community cooking suggestions, page 235).

PACKAGE MEALS TO GIVE AWAY?
If the recipe calls for a baking dish, you can use your own glass or metal pans. But if you decide to give a meal away, it can be a bother for both you and the recipient to worry about the container's return. In that case, you may wish to use a disposable foil pan. Think about the intended use of the meals you choose and plan to package them accordingly.

MIX MARINADES?
Many of the marinades can be made in a large, clear liquid measuring cup instead of a bowl. This will help take the guesswork out when dividing the sauce among the bags.

PREVENT ICE CRYSTALS?
Remove as much air as possible from each bag before sealing and placing it in the freezer. This will increase the freezer life of the food and keep ice crystals from forming.

When filling freezer bags with sauce, it helps to place your bag in a large tub to keep it stable and avoid spills.

AVOID LEAKS?

If you're packaging meat with bones, such as pork chops or ribs, double-bag the freezer meal to help avoid leaks. Simply fill the first freezer bag and seal it. Then place the sealed bag inside a second bag. Label the outer bag.

KEEP TRACK OF WHAT'S IN THE FREEZER?

Keep a freezer inventory. Maintain it so you know at a glance what you have and where it is in the freezer. To keep track of the contents of your freezer, you may want to use the Freezer Inventory form on page 240.

POUR SAUCE INTO FREEZER BAGS?

This can be a messy procedure. Here's what we've found works best: Save cracker boxes, large plastic sour cream or cottage cheese tubs, or the enormous #10 cans (such as those used in the Basic Red Sauce recipe), being careful to leave a smooth edge when removing the lid. Put the freezer bag inside one of these containers and fold the top of the bag over the rim of the container. This will hold your bag open and prevent spills while you measure or pour in ingredients.

CORRECTING MISTAKES

Every once in a while you'll discover you've made a mistake while preparing a recipe. Don't panic! In all our years of cooking for our families and with groups in our businesses, we've encountered only a few mistakes that couldn't be fixed. The rest we were able to repair — and in some cases, we preferred the "wrong" version!

We've designed our method to help you avoid mistakes in the first place. We've tested for how intense the seasonings taste, how reliably an entrée comes together in your kitchen, and how well it retains its quality in the freezer. Nevertheless, mistakes still happen, and to avoid having to throw away food, here are some suggestions in case you face a kitchen quandary. (See more on page 234.)

HOW CAN I FIX MY RECIPE IF I . . .

MEASURE AN INGREDIENT INCORRECTLY?

If you add too much of one ingredient, often you can simply increase the whole recipe proportionately. See our tips on adapting recipes (page 234) for some rules of thumb.

If you put too much of a dry ingredient into a mix and it's sitting on top of other ingredients or floating on top of a marinade, try to scoop off the excess. Chances are, you'll be able to approximate the original amount.

FORGET TO INCLUDE AN INGREDIENT?

If you're all finished and find an unused ingredient on the counter, determine where you made the error and whether or not it will be easy to add. In a marinade, for example, you can simply add the correct amount to each bag before freezing. Alternatively, you can add it to the entrée when it comes out of the freezer, but remember to make a note of it on the label.

BUY THE WRONG MEAT?

Sometimes you'll find you end up with a cut of meat you didn't mean to buy. The package may have been placed in the wrong section of the cooler and picked up inadvertently. One of our customers accidentally bought pork instead of beef for the Beef Barley Soup. She ended up making Pork Barley Soup and it was great. If the recipe can be adapted for the cut of meat, go ahead and use it anyway; otherwise, just pick another recipe to use with the meat that you took home.

FIND SOMETHING TOO SALTY?

Salt is an ingredient that intensifies in strength in the freezer. We write our recipes to account for this, but different brands of bouillon or base and other seasonings can vary in saltiness. Individual tastes differ, too. If a sauce or marinade tastes too salty to you before it goes into the freezer, you can make the sauce again, this time omitting all salt or bouillon/base that the recipe calls for. Mix the two sauces together. You can use the same method for a marinade, or you can add plain chicken broth or apple juice a teaspoonful at a time until the saltiness has been diluted. *Please don't taste sauces or marinades that contain raw meat!*

FIND THERE'S TOO MUCH FLAVOR?

Like salt, vinegar and alcohol can impart a strong, pronounced flavor. If you decide there's too strong a vinegar or alcohol flavor for your taste, adding plain chicken broth, apple juice, or water will help balance the dish.

FIND THERE'S NOT ENOUGH FLAVOR?

If you taste something before it goes into the freezer and think its flavor should be stronger, resist the temptation to doctor the seasonings. Many flavors intensify in the freezer. If you need to, you can adjust the seasoning when you cook the entrée.

BREAK OR TEAR A FREEZER BAG?

Breakage is rare, and there are simple ways to keep your freezer bags intact. Hot sauces can weaken a freezer bag: That's another reason we advise you to always cool food before placing it in a bag. Bags full of sauce or soup tend to freeze into very hard packages that can break open, so it's best to move them very little once they're frozen.

If you damage a bag before a meal has been frozen, carefully transfer the contents to a new freezer bag. If you discover a tear in a bag after the food has been frozen, put the whole meal, broken bag and all, into a new freezer bag.

FORGET TO PUT FOOD INTO THE REFRIGERATOR/ FREEZER?

This one can be a heartbreaker. We've heard a few stories from cooks who inadvertently left a freezer meal on the counter too long. Perishable food must be stored at a temperature below 40°F (4°C) or it is considered unsafe to consume. Please do not risk your health. Throw away any food that has not been held at a safe temperature.

PREVENTING FREEZER BURN

The result of moisture loss from poorly packaged food, freezer burn creates a fuzzy and grayish white surface on the frozen item. It's not harmful, but it can result in an undesirable flavor and texture. Prevent freezer burn by following our freezing tips.

Ice crystals are different from freezer burn. Their appearance has to do with how quickly the food has frozen. A freezer that's too cold will create small ice crystals, and the smaller the crystals, the less they will diminish food quality. The ideal freezer temperature is between −5 and 0°F (−21 and −18°C).

RECIPE

USE BY
7/10

...Broccoli Bake

CHICKEN
MAIN DISHES

- Place ...dish
  Sprinkle with cheese + bread
  crumbs
- Bake: uncovered 35-40 min or bubbling

CHERRY
SKILLET CHICKEN

MAKES 3 freezer meals, 2 breast halves each

INGREDIENTS

6	individual boneless, skinless chicken breast halves
1½	cups chopped dried sweet cherries (about 9 ounces)
¾	cup hot water
6	tablespoons white balsamic vinegar
¼	cup tart cherry juice
1	tablespoon sugar
1	teaspoon sea salt

ON HAND FOR COOKING EACH FREEZER MEAL

2	tablespoons vegetable oil
½	cup water

PACK IT UP

Waxed paper

Three 1-gallon freezer bags, labeled

This chicken is excellent chopped over salad with red grapes, blue cheese or Gorgonzola, and sunflower seeds. Consider dressing the salad with our Raspberry Vinaigrette (page 208). — KN

---

1 Trim chicken as desired.

2 Lay each piece of chicken, smooth side down, between two sheets of waxed paper. Using a rolling pin or a meat tenderizer, pound each chicken piece to 1 inch thick. Divide chicken evenly among freezer bags.

3 Place cherries in a food processor and cover with hot water. Let stand for 5 minutes.

4 Measure vinegar, cherry juice, sugar, and salt into food processor. Combine well with cherry mixture.

5 Divide cherry sauce equally into freezer bags with chicken. Seal and gently shake bag to distribute sauce.

6 Seal and freeze. Food will stay at optimal quality for up to 3 months in freezer.

TO COOK ONE FREEZER MEAL

1 Completely thaw one freezer meal in refrigerator.

2 In a large skillet, heat oil over medium heat. Add chicken and cook until it begins to brown, about 3 minutes on each side.

3 As chicken cooks, measure ½ cup water into bag with remaining cherry sauce. Combine and set aside.

4 Reduce heat to medium-low and pour cherry sauce over chicken. Cover and simmer until an instant-read thermometer inserted into thickest part of chicken reads 165°F (74°C), 12 to 15 minutes.

NOTE: Consider substituting dry white wine in place of water when cooking this entrée, if desired. It's a subtle change that brings out different flavors.

CHICKEN CORDON BLEU

MAKES 3 freezer meals, 4 servings each

Chicken, ham, and cheese — what's not to like? When my oldest three girls were very young, they would split one of these three ways: Ellen ate the chicken, Laura ate the ham, and Natalie ate the cheese! — LA

1 Trim chicken as desired.

2 Lay out three shallow dishes. Measure flour into one, eggs into another, and breadcrumbs into the third.

3 Lay each piece of chicken, smooth side down, between two sheets of waxed paper. Using a rolling pin or a meat tenderizer, pound each chicken piece to ½ inch thick. Take one piece of chicken, coat with flour, dip in egg, and then coat with breadcrumbs. Set aside. Repeat with remaining chicken pieces. Discard remaining flour, egg, and breadcrumbs.

4 Fold one piece of cheese into a small bundle and place in the middle of one slice of ham. Fold sides of ham in, enveloping cheese. Place a bundle on the narrow end of a breaded chicken piece, roll chicken into a packet, and secure tightly by wrapping with plastic wrap. Repeat with remaining cheese, ham, and chicken. Divide chicken rolls evenly among freezer bags.

5 Seal and freeze. Food will stay at optimal quality for up to 3 months in freezer.

TO COOK ONE FREEZER MEAL

1 Remove desired number of chicken rolls from freezer. Discard plastic wrap while chicken is still frozen and place rolls in a greased baking dish. Place in refrigerator to thaw completely.

2 Preheat oven to 350°F (180°C).

3 Brush each chicken roll with 2 teaspoons melted butter and bake for 45 minutes, or until an instant-read thermometer inserted into thickest part of chicken reads 165°F (74°C).

TOOTHPICKS?

I don't recommend securing the bundles with toothpicks because they don't seal these up tightly enough to prevent the cheese from leaking out. When secured snugly in plastic wrap, each bundle should stay together on its own when it comes out of the freezer.

INGREDIENTS

- 6 pounds boneless, skinless chicken breast halves (about 12 halves)
- 1 cup all-purpose flour
- 4 eggs, lightly beaten
- 2 cups dry breadcrumbs
- 12 slices Swiss cheese
- 12 slices deli ham

ON HAND FOR COOKING EACH FREEZER MEAL

- 2 teaspoons melted butter per chicken roll

PACK IT UP

Waxed paper

Plastic wrap

Three 1-gallon freezer bags, labeled

CHICKEN-BROCCOLI BAKE

MAKES 3 freezer meals, 4–6 servings each

This is based on a favorite casserole I used to make with cream of chicken soup. My condensed soup days are over, so I rewrote the recipe to include a sauce from scratch. Serve over brown basmati rice for extra nutrition. — LA

1 Trim chicken as desired and cut into bite-size pieces. In a large skillet, cook chicken over medium heat until no longer pink, about 30 minutes. Remove from heat and cool. Divide cooled chicken evenly among three unlabeled 1-gallon freezer bags.

2 While chicken cools, melt butter in a separate large saucepan over medium heat. Add mushrooms and sauté until softened, about 5 minutes. Add flour and stir. The mixture will be lumpy. Cook, stirring, for 2 minutes. Add chicken base, curry powder, and pepper; stir. Gradually add water and milk. Cook, stirring constantly, until sauce thickens, about 10 minutes. Whisk to make a smooth sauce. Add lemon juice only after sauce has thickened. Cool sauce.

3 Divide cooled sauce evenly over chicken. Measure 2 cups of broccoli pieces into each bag of chicken and sauce. Seal bags.

4 Measure 2 cups cheese and ½ cup breadcrumbs into each 1-quart freezer bag. Seal bags.

5 Place one bag of chicken/broccoli and one bag of cheese/breadcrumb mixture into each labeled 1-gallon bag.

6 Seal and freeze. Food will stay at optimal quality for up to 2 months in freezer.

TO COOK ONE FREEZER MEAL

1 Completely thaw one freezer meal in refrigerator.

2 Preheat oven to 350°F (180°C).

3 Place chicken and broccoli mixture in an ungreased baking dish and sprinkle with cheese and breadcrumbs. Bake, uncovered, for 35 to 40 minutes, or until sauce is bubbling and cheese is melted.

INGREDIENTS

- 6 pounds boneless, skinless chicken breast halves (about 12 halves)
- ½ cup (1 stick) butter
- 1 pound fresh white mushrooms, cleaned and sliced
- ¾ cup all-purpose flour
- 1 tablespoon chicken base
- 1 tablespoon curry powder
- ¾ teaspoon black pepper
- 2 cups water
- 4 cups milk
- 2 tablespoons lemon juice
- 6 cups broccoli pieces (about 1¼ pounds), washed
- 6 cups shredded cheddar cheese (about 1½ pounds)
- 1½ cups dry breadcrumbs

> **PACK IT UP**
> *Six 1-gallon freezer bags; label 3*
> *Three 1-quart freezer bags*

CHICKEN CURRY

MAKES 3 freezer meals, 4–6 servings each

This mild and creamy curry is a hit with everyone. If you're not sure whether your family will eat curry, I suggest you start here. Serve over your favorite rice. — LA

INGREDIENTS

- 6 pounds boneless, skinless chicken breast halves (about 12 halves)
- 1 cup (2 sticks) butter
- 2 cups chopped onion (about 2 medium)
- ¼ cup curry powder
- 2 tablespoons chicken base
- 2 tablespoons minced garlic
- 2 tablespoons minced ginger
- 2 tablespoons sugar
- 2 teaspoons salt
- 1 cup all-purpose flour
- 4 cups milk
- 4 cups water
- 2 tablespoons lemon juice

1 Trim chicken as desired and cut into bite-size pieces. In a large skillet, cook chicken over medium heat until no longer pink, about 30 minutes. Remove from heat and cool. Divide cooled chicken evenly among freezer bags.

2 While chicken cools, melt butter in a separate large saucepan over medium heat. Add onion and cook, stirring, until soft, about 5 minutes. Add curry powder, chicken base, garlic, ginger, sugar, and salt, and cook, stirring, for 2 minutes. Add flour and cook, stirring, 2 minutes longer. Mixture will be like a paste. Gradually add milk and water; cook, stirring constantly, until sauce has thickened. Whisk to make a smooth sauce. Add lemon juice only after sauce has thickened. Cool sauce.

3 Divide cooled sauce evenly over chicken.

4 Seal and freeze. Food will stay at optimal quality for up to 2 months in freezer.

TO COOK ONE FREEZER MEAL

1 Completely thaw one freezer meal in refrigerator.

2 In a large skillet, bring chicken and curry sauce to a simmer over medium heat and cook until heated through. Do not boil.

PACK IT UP

Three 1-gallon freezer bags, labeled

ACCOMPANIMENTS FOR CURRY

Offer a variety of toppings so everyone can select their favorite flavors to sprinkle over dinner. The platter could include toasted coconut, toasted almonds, fresh apple pieces, pineapple tidbits, raisins, dried cranberries, chopped scallions, mango chutney, hot chili paste, and/ or sweet chili sauce.

MARIACHI
CHICKEN ROLLS

MAKES 3 freezer meals, 4 servings each

These rolls are perfect as a main dish on their own or as a potluck contribution, with each piece cut into four smaller pieces after cooking. Complement the dish with a fresh citrus-jicama fruit salad.

1 In a small bowl, combine pepper, scallions, and olives. Set aside.

2 In a large bowl and using an electric mixer, blend cream cheese and salsa. Set aside.

3 Trim chicken as desired. Lay each piece of chicken, smooth side down, on a cutting board. Using your palm, press down on thickest part of chicken. Place 2 tablespoons of pepper mixture near widest end of each chicken piece. Starting with widest part of breast, roll a chicken piece around filling. Repeat with remaining chicken pieces. Divide rolls among three greased baking dishes.

4 Divide cream cheese mixture evenly over each dish of chicken. Sprinkle with paprika to taste.

5 Wrap each dish entirely in plastic wrap. Top with foil, label, and freeze. Food will stay at optimal quality for up to 2 months in freezer.

TO COOK ONE FREEZER MEAL

1 Completely thaw one freezer meal in refrigerator.

2 Preheat oven to 350°F (180°C).

3 Remove foil and plastic wrap from baking dish and replace foil. Bake, covered, for 1 hour, or until an instant-read thermometer inserted into center of a roll reads 165°F (74°C).

INGREDIENTS

- 1 large red bell pepper, diced
- 4 scallions, chopped
- 1 (2¼-ounce) can chopped black olives (about ½ cup)
- 3 (8-ounce) packages light cream cheese, cubed and softened
- 3 cups prepared salsa
- 6 pounds boneless, skinless chicken breast halves (about 12 halves)

  Paprika

PACK IT UP

Three 8-inch square baking dishes, greased

Plastic wrap

Aluminum foil

CHICKEN PARMIGIANA

MAKES 3 freezer meals, 4 servings each

INGREDIENTS

6   pounds boneless, skinless chicken breast halves (about 12 halves)

1   cup all-purpose flour

4   eggs, lightly beaten

2   cups dry breadcrumbs

12 slices mozzarella cheese

6   cups Basic Red Sauce (page 190)

Many recipes for this dish call for frying the chicken. I find that messy and time consuming, so I developed this baked version. This entrée pairs nicely with your favorite pasta and a little extra red sauce. — LA

1 Trim chicken as desired. Lay out three shallow dishes. Measure flour into one, eggs into another, and breadcrumbs into the third.

2 Lay each piece of chicken, smooth side down, on a cutting board. Using your palm, press down on thickest part of chicken. Take one piece of chicken, coat with flour, dip in egg, and then coat with breadcrumbs. Repeat with remaining chicken pieces. Place coated chicken in one layer on a rimmed baking sheet.

3 When all chicken is coated, place in freezer for 1 hour. Discard remaining flour, egg, and breadcrumbs.

4 Into each 1-quart freezer bag, measure 2 cups red sauce. Seal.

5 Divide cheese into three portions of 4 slices each; wrap in plastic wrap. Divide frozen chicken evenly among 1-gallon freezer bags and layer a piece of waxed or parchment paper between each piece of chicken. Place one bag of sauce and one packet of cheese into each bag of chicken.

6 Seal and freeze. Food will stay at optimal quality for up to 3 months in freezer.

TO COOK ONE FREEZER MEAL

1 Completely thaw one freezer meal in refrigerator.

2 Preheat oven to 375°F (190°C).

3 Place chicken in a greased baking dish. Bake, uncovered, for 20 minutes. Pour red sauce evenly over each piece of chicken and continue baking for 10 minutes longer, or until an instant-read thermometer inserted into thickest part of chicken reads 165°F (74°C). Place a slice of cheese on top of each piece of chicken and bake until melted.

PACK IT UP

Three 1-quart freezer bags

Plastic wrap

Three 1-gallon freezer bags, labeled

Waxed paper or parchment paper

DAVE'S SWAMP BLUES
BARBECUED CHICKEN

MAKES 3 freezer meals, 4 servings each

INGREDIENTS

- 2 teaspoons vegetable oil
- 1 cup chopped onion (about 1 medium)
- 2¼ cups ketchup
- ½ cup water
- ¼ cup bourbon
- 2 tablespoons lime juice
- 4 teaspoons jerk seasoning (such as Penzeys, or try our homemade version, below)
- 1 tablespoon smoked paprika
- 1 tablespoon firmly packed brown sugar
- 6 pounds boneless, skinless chicken breast halves (about 12 halves)

PACK IT UP

Three 1-gallon freezer bags, labeled

I was working on a new barbecue sauce in the kitchen one Sunday afternoon when the radio program *This American Life* was playing swamp blues. I happened upon the right mix of ingredients to create a tangy new sauce. It was just the right thing for just the right lazy summer day. Following this recipe are two more that use this barbecued chicken as the main ingredient. — KN

1 In a large saucepan, heat oil over medium heat. Add onion and cook, stirring, until soft, 2 to 3 minutes. Stir in ketchup, water, bourbon, lime juice, jerk seasoning, paprika, and sugar. Reduce heat and simmer for 30 minutes, stirring frequently. Cool sauce.

2 While sauce is cooling, trim chicken as desired. Divide chicken evenly among freezer bags. Divide cooled sauce evenly over chicken. Gently shake each bag to combine contents.

3 Seal and freeze. Food will stay at optimal quality for up to 3 months in freezer.

TO COOK ONE FREEZER MEAL

1 Completely thaw one freezer meal in refrigerator.

2 Prepare a medium-low fire in a gas or charcoal grill.

3 Grill chicken, turning every 5 minutes and basting frequently with marinade, for 30 minutes, or until an instant-read thermometer inserted into thickest part of chicken reads 165°F (74°C). Do not baste chicken during last 5 minutes of grilling.

HOMEMADE JERK SEASONING

Making your own jerk seasoning is as easy as mixing together the following spices: 1 teaspoon ground allspice, 1 teaspoon cayenne pepper, ½ teaspoon black pepper, ½ teaspoon ground cinnamon, ½ teaspoon ground nutmeg, ½ teaspoon dried thyme.

DAVE'S
SKILLET HASH

MAKES 6–8 servings

I tried this recipe out on my dad several times before getting it right. My grandma used to make hash for him and his three brothers when he was a boy. Grandma's cooking was legendary in the family as well as in her township, where she and Grandpa Bill ran a tavern and eatery. I'm sure this hash isn't as good as hers — it's hard to compete with a son's memory of his mother's fine cooking, after all. Yet Dave's Skillet Hash has managed to win his approval. — KN

1 In a deep skillet or Dutch oven, heat oil over medium heat. Add potatoes and cook, stirring frequently, for 10 minutes. Add onion and green and red bell peppers, and cook, stirring, for 5 minutes longer. Pour in broth. Sprinkle in black pepper, salt, paprika, and red pepper flakes, and stir to combine.

2 Reduce heat, cover, and cook, stirring frequently, until the potatoes are soft, 10 to 15 minutes. Add chicken, re-cover pan, and cook 5 minutes longer. Top with cheese, re-cover pan, and serve when cheese is melted.

PREP AHEAD

2 Dave's Swamp Blues Barbecued Chicken breast halves, grilled and chopped (page 28)

INGREDIENTS

1 tablespoon grapeseed oil

3½ cups (uncooked) cubed potatoes (about 1¼ pounds)

1 cup chopped onion (about 1 medium)

½ cup chopped green bell pepper

½ cup chopped red bell pepper

¾ cup chicken broth

1 teaspoon black pepper

½ teaspoon salt

½ teaspoon smoked paprika

¼ teaspoon red pepper flakes

¾ cup shredded cheddar cheese (about 3 ounces)

FAMILY MATTERS

My Uncle Dave passed away in early 2005. I learned of his passing minutes before we met to work on the first edition of this book. He loved to cook, too. I managed to rescue his Penzeys spice collection before it landed in the trash. Uncle Dave is the person who introduced me to Penzeys spices. The jerk seasoning I used in this recipe went straight from his cupboard to mine as my "inheritance." And so I dedicate this chicken recipe to my Uncle Dave, who called me "sparrow legs," tricked me into eating squirrel and rabbit, loved Elvis, cooked well, endured so much, and was loved by many. Including me.

DAVE'S BARBECUED
CHICKEN PIZZA

MAKES 6–8 servings

I prefer homemade pizza over store-bought because you can customize your ingredients and dough. There are many options! Just be sure to get enough dough to cover a 16-inch round or a standard 15- by 10-inch baking sheet. — KN

PREP AHEAD

2 Dave's Swamp Blues Barbecued Chicken breast halves, grilled and thinly sliced (page 28)

INGREDIENTS

1 pizza dough (about 24 ounces)

½ cup pizza sauce (try our homemade version on page 192)

1 tablespoon smoke-flavored barbecue sauce

3½ cups shredded mozzarella cheese (about 14 ounces)

½ cup shredded Cotija cheese (about 2 ounces)

1 Preheat oven to 400°F (200°C).

2 Roll dough to desired shape and size. In a small bowl, mix pizza sauce and barbecue sauce; spread over dough. Discard any remaining sauce or save it for another use.

3 Spread mozzarella over sauce; top with chicken and sprinkle with Cotija.

4 Bake pizza for 15 to 18 minutes, or until crust is golden brown and mozzarella is melted.

COTIJA CHEESE

Often compared to feta cheese because of its tangy flavor, Cotija is a common ingredient in Mexican cooking. You're likely to find it near the deli in the specialty cheese case.

MOLASSES-RUM CHICKEN

MAKES 3 freezer meals, 4 servings each

This dish retains the distinctive flavor of the liquor after it is cooked. If you prefer more subtle flavors, consider cutting the rum in half. I serve this with a fruit salad featuring red grapes, pineapple, mango, or peaches. — KN

1 Trim chicken as desired. Divide chicken evenly among freezer bags.

2 In a large bowl, combine rum, barbecue sauce, lime juice, molasses, hot pepper sauce, oil, and salt. Divide marinade evenly over chicken.

3 Seal and gently shake each bag to combine contents. Freeze. Food will stay at optimal quality for up to 3 months in freezer.

TO COOK ONE FREEZER MEAL

1 Completely thaw one freezer meal in refrigerator.

2 Prepare a medium-low fire in a gas or charcoal grill.

3 Grill chicken, turning occasionally, for 30 minutes, or until an instant-read thermometer inserted into thickest part of chicken reads 165°F (74°C). Discard remaining marinade.

INGREDIENTS

- 6 pounds boneless, skinless chicken breast halves (about 12 halves)
- 1½ cups blackstrap rum (such as Cruzan) or other dark rum
- ¾ cup prepared barbecue sauce
- ⅔ cup lime juice
- 3 tablespoons molasses
- 3 tablespoons hot pepper sauce
- 2 tablespoons vegetable oil
- 1 tablespoon salt

> **PACK IT UP**
> *Three 1-gallon freezer bags, labeled*

MANGO-CRANBERRY CHICKEN

MAKES 4 freezer meals, 4 servings each

INGREDIENTS

- 6 pounds boneless, skinless chicken breast halves (about 12 halves)
- ½ cup chopped dried mango (about 4 ounces)
- ¼ cup dried cranberries
- ⅔ cup boiling water
- 2 (9-ounce) jars mango chutney (about 2 cups)
- ½ cup rice vinegar
- ¼ cup minced onion
- 1 tablespoon minced garlic
- 1 tablespoon toasted sesame oil
- 1 tablespoon curry powder

Of all the dishes I cook, this is one of my favorites. It's easy to prepare and mild enough for children to enjoy, too. Serve this curry over rice or noodles and top with any of the accompaniments listed on page 24. — KN

1 Trim chicken and cut into bite-size strips. Divide chicken evenly among freezer bags.

2 In a medium bowl, stir together mango, cranberries, and boiling water. Stir in chutney, vinegar, onion, garlic, sesame oil, and curry powder. Cool sauce. Divide cooled sauce evenly over chicken.

3 Seal bags and freeze. Food will stay at optimal quality for up to 3 months in freezer.

TO COOK ONE FREEZER MEAL

1 Completely thaw one freezer meal in refrigerator.

2 In a large skillet, simmer chicken and sauce over medium heat until meat is thoroughly cooked, 15 to 20 minutes.

PACK IT UP

Four 1-gallon freezer bags, labeled

PECAN-CRUSTED
CHICKEN STRIPS

MAKES 3 freezer meals, about 12 strips each

These chicken strips especially appeal to kids. Try any leftover chicken strips chopped and served over salad with candied pecans, blue cheese, and honey mustard dressing.

1 Trim chicken as desired. Cut each breast half lengthwise into three strips. Divide chicken evenly among three unlabeled 1-gallon freezer bags.

2 In a medium bowl, combine mustard, honey, oil, salt, garlic, and pepper. Divide sauce evenly over chicken. Seal bags.

3 Into each 1-quart freezer bag, measure 1 cup panko and ½ cup pecans; seal. Place one bag of chicken and one bag of breadcrumb mixture into each labeled 1-gallon bag.

4 Seal and freeze. Food will stay at optimal quality for up to 3 months in freezer.

TO COOK ONE FREEZER MEAL

1 Completely thaw one freezer meal in refrigerator.

2 Preheat oven to 350°F (180°C).

3 Place breadcrumb mixture on a plate. Shake excess sauce off each piece of chicken, roll in crumbs, and place on a greased baking sheet.

4 Bake for 30 minutes (or 20 minutes if using smaller chicken pieces as pictured at left), or until chicken pulls apart easily and is no longer pink in thickest part and crust is golden.

INGREDIENTS

- 6 pounds boneless, skinless chicken breast halves (about 12 halves)
- ¾ cup spicy brown mustard
- 1⅓ cups honey
- ½ cup olive oil
- 2 teaspoons salt
- 2 teaspoons granulated garlic
- 2 teaspoons black pepper
- 3 cups panko (Japanese-style breadcrumbs)
- 1½ cups pecans (8 ounces), finely ground

PACK IT UP

Six 1-gallon freezer bags; label 3

Three 1-quart freezer bags

PORT
BARBECUED CHICKEN

MAKES 3 freezer meals, 4 servings each

The delicious homemade barbecue sauce in this dish, featuring port, offers more complex flavors than most other barbecue sauces. Feel free to pump up the zip by adding more red pepper flakes. Try this chicken in our Chicken Salad with Port Barbecue Sauce (page 38) and on our Chicken Pizza with Port Barbecue Sauce (page 39). — KN

INGREDIENTS

- ½ cup (1 stick) butter
- 5 ounces shallots, minced (about 1 cup)
- 1½ tablespoons dry mustard
- 1½ teaspoons red pepper flakes
- 2 cups ketchup
- ¾ cup Worcestershire sauce
- ⅓ cup port
- ⅓ cup water
- ½ cup firmly packed dark brown sugar
- ¼ cup soy sauce
- 1 tablespoon molasses
- 6 pounds boneless, skinless chicken breast halves (about 12 halves)

1 In a large saucepan, melt butter over medium heat. Add shallots and cook, stirring, for 5 minutes. Add dry mustard and pepper flakes; cook, stirring, until shallots are tender, about 2 minutes. Add ketchup, Worcestershire, port, water, sugar, soy sauce, and molasses. Bring to a boil; reduce heat and simmer, stirring frequently, for 20 minutes. Cool sauce.

2 While sauce is cooling, trim chicken as desired. Divide chicken evenly among freezer bags. Divide cooled sauce evenly over chicken. Seal and gently shake each bag to combine contents.

3 Freeze. Food will stay at optimal quality for up to 3 months in freezer.

TO COOK ONE FREEZER MEAL

1 Completely thaw one freezer meal in refrigerator.

2 Prepare a medium-low fire in a gas or charcoal grill.

3 Grill chicken, turning every 5 minutes and basting frequently with the marinade, for 30 minutes, or until an instant-read thermometer inserted into thickest part of chicken reads 165°F (74°C). Do not baste chicken during last 5 minutes of grilling.

4 Boil remaining sauce for at least 5 minutes if you wish to serve it with chicken.

PACK IT UP

Three 1-gallon freezer bags, labeled

SHALLOTS

You can find shallots near the onions and garlic in your grocery store's produce section. Some people find the flavor of shallots to be a cross between a mild, sweet onion and garlic. Minced shallots will also add wonderful flavor to your favorite vinaigrette.

CHICKEN SALAD
WITH PORT BARBECUE SAUCE

MAKES 4 servings

PREP AHEAD

2 Port Barbecue Chicken breast halves, grilled and thinly sliced (page 36)

INGREDIENTS

1 tablespoon butter

1 onion, cut in half and thinly sliced

½ teaspoon honey

2 large hearts of romaine, rinsed and torn into bite-size pieces

1 cup black beans, rinsed and drained

1 cup frozen roasted corn

2 Roma tomatoes, quartered lengthwise

1 avocado, pitted, peeled, and cut into 8 wedges

½ cup ranch dressing

½ cup honey barbecue sauce

When I lived in the Seattle area, I enjoyed trying all kinds of new restaurants and pubs. I came across a barbecued-chicken salad at one local restaurant that kept me coming back. I created this recipe to mimic the flavors in that memorable dish. — KN

1 In a small skillet, melt butter over medium-low heat. Add onion and brown slowly, stirring occasionally, until caramelized, about 20 minutes. Stir in honey and cook for 5 minutes. Set aside to cool.

2 Place one-quarter of lettuce on each of four plates. Top lettuce with ¼ cup black beans, ¼ cup corn, one-quarter of chicken, one-quarter of caramelized onion, 2 tomato slices, and 2 avocado wedges.

3 Set out ranch dressing and barbecue sauce, allowing each person to use and combine dressings as desired. You may wish to thin the ranch a bit with water so that it pours easily and can be combined with the barbecue sauce.

CHICKEN PIZZA
WITH PORT BARBECUE SAUCE

MAKES 6–8 servings

Gourmet pizzas from restaurants are at least four times more expensive than those you can make at home. Experimenting can be fun and tasty too! Just be sure to get enough dough to cover a 16-inch round or a standard 15- by 10-inch baking sheet. Accompany this pizza with a crisp green salad. — KN

1 Preheat oven to 400°F (200°C).

2 Roll dough to desired shape and size. In a small bowl, mix pizza sauce and barbecue sauce; spread over dough.

3 Spread mozzarella over sauce; top with chicken and sprinkle with Asiago.

4 Bake pizza for 15 to 18 minutes, or until crust is golden brown and mozzarella is melted.

PREP AHEAD

2 Port Barbecue Chicken breast halves, grilled and thinly sliced (page 36)

INGREDIENTS

1 pizza dough (about 24 ounces)

½ cup pizza sauce (try our homemade version on page 192)

1 tablespoon honey barbecue sauce

3½ cups shredded mozzarella cheese (about 14 ounces)

½ cup shredded Asiago cheese (about 1½ ounces)

SUN-DRIED
PESTO CHICKEN

MAKES 3 freezer meals, 4 servings each

With my kids now entering college, they are sometimes home and sometimes not. They sometimes bring friends for dinner and sometimes not. Sometimes they need to "shop" from my freezer to cover dinner during busy times of transition. I package this recipe in smaller portions by making six freezer meals with two servings each. That way, I can grab exactly what I need. — KN

1 Trim chicken as desired into 12 portions. Divide chicken evenly among freezer bags.

2 In the bowl of a food processor, pulse tomatoes and garlic until a thick paste forms.

3 Transfer tomato mixture into a medium bowl. Add wine, basil, pepper, salt, and sugar, and stir to combine. Divide sauce evenly over chicken.

4 Seal and gently shake each bag to combine contents. Freeze. Food will stay at optimal quality for up to 3 months in freezer.

TO COOK ONE FREEZER MEAL

1 Completely thaw one freezer meal in refrigerator.

2 Preheat oven to 350°F (180°C).

3 Place chicken breasts into an 8-inch square baking dish and top with remaining marinade. Cover with aluminum foil and bake for 35 minutes. Remove foil and bake for 10 minutes longer, or until an instant-read thermometer inserted into thickest part of chicken reads 165°F (74°C). Spoon sauce over top of chicken to moisten before serving, if needed.

INGREDIENTS

- 6 pounds boneless, skinless chicken breast halves (about 12 halves)
- 1 cup drained, oil-packed sun-dried tomatoes
- 6 garlic cloves, peeled and coarsely chopped
- ½ cup dry white wine
- 1 teaspoon dried basil
- 1 teaspoon black pepper
- 1 teaspoon salt
- 1 teaspoon sugar

PACK IT UP
Three 1-gallon freezer bags, labeled

CHICKEN ROLLS
WITH CRISPY ALMOND-RYE BREADING

MAKES 3 freezer meals, 4 servings each

INGREDIENTS

- 12 rye crispbread (such as Wasa) crackers

- ¾ cup smoked almonds

- 6 pounds boneless, skinless chicken breast halves (about 12 halves)

- 3 egg whites, lightly beaten

- 1 (8-ounce) package cream cheese

As a practical, everyday cook, I usually don't bother with fancy food. But if I'm expecting special dinner guests, these rolls are great to have on hand. Since they are flash frozen, I can make up a batch and then pull them out a day or so before my event as the RSVPs roll in. Cream cheese is a mild filling that appeals to many, but feel free to experiment with other spreadable cheeses, such as Boursin. — KN

---

1 In a food processor, pulse crispbread and almonds until finely ground.

2 Trim chicken as desired. Lay out two shallow dishes. Place crispbread mixture in one dish. To keep breading from absorbing excess moisture from eggs, pour half of breading mixture into a small bowl and set aside; use this to refill the shallow breading dish as it empties. Put egg whites in a second dish.

3 Working with 4 to 6 breast halves at a time, lay each piece of chicken, smooth side down, between two sheets of waxed paper. Pound chicken to ½ inch thickness with a rolling pin or meat tenderizer. Note the number of chicken pieces. Set chicken aside.

4 Slice cream cheese block lengthwise into two long strips, then cut strips into cubes equal to number of chicken pieces.

5 Spread one cream cheese cube on each piece of chicken. Starting from widest end of each breast half, roll chicken piece and secure end with a toothpick. Dip chicken into egg whites, then roll through breadcrumb mixture until well covered. Place each chicken roll on a rimmed baking sheet. Discard remaining egg and breading.

6 Place coated chicken rolls in freezer for 1 hour. Divide frozen rolls evenly among double-bagged freezer bags. Seal and return to freezer. Food will stay at optimal quality for up to 3 months in freezer.

PACK IT UP

Waxed paper

12–14 toothpicks

Six 1-gallon freezer bags, double bagged; label 3

TO COOK ONE FREEZER MEAL

1 Remove rolls from freezer and place in a greased 9-inch square baking dish. Cover and place in refrigerator to thaw completely.

2 Preheat oven to 350°F (180°C).

3 Bake, uncovered, for 45 to 60 minutes, or until an instant-read thermometer inserted into thickest part of a roll reads 165°F (74°C).

SWEET
ASIAN CHICKEN

MAKES 3 freezer meals, 4 servings each

This recipe is based on several recipes and is the culmination of years of experimentation. At the time I created it, a friend was lending me copies of *Bon Appétit* and *Gourmet* magazines. This was in the prechildren phase of my life, when I had the time to read often. My inspiration likely came from these sources, and the recipe was cultivated through years of feedback from my family. Children particularly enjoy the sweet Asian flavors of this marinated chicken breast. Serve with soba noodles or rice and sweet Asian coleslaw. — KN

1 Trim chicken as desired. Divide chicken evenly among freezer bags.

2 In a medium bowl, combine soy sauce, sugar, lime juice, and curry powder. Divide marinade evenly over chicken.

3 Into each bag, measure 1 tablespoon minced garlic and ¾ teaspoon pepper flakes.

4 Seal and gently shake each bag to combine contents. Freeze. Food will stay at optimal quality for up to 3 months in freezer.

TO COOK ONE FREEZER MEAL

Completely thaw one freezer meal in refrigerator. This entrée can be prepared outdoors on a grill or in the kitchen on your stovetop.

For Outdoor Cooking

1 Prepare a medium-low fire in a gas or charcoal grill.

2 Grill chicken, turning every 5 minutes and basting frequently with marinade, for 30 minutes, or until an instant-read thermometer inserted into thickest part of chicken reads 165°F (74°C). Do not baste chicken during last 5 minutes of grilling. Discard remaining marinade.

For Indoor Cooking

Cut marinated chicken into ½-inch strips. In a wok or large skillet, heat oil. Stir-fry chicken over medium heat until pieces pull apart easily and are no longer pink in the center, about 25 minutes.

INGREDIENTS

- 6 pounds boneless, skinless chicken breast halves (about 12 halves)
- 1 cup soy sauce
- 1 cup firmly packed brown sugar
- ¼ cup lime juice
- ½ teaspoon curry powder
- 3 tablespoons minced garlic
- 2¼ teaspoons red pepper flakes

ON HAND FOR COOKING EACH FREEZER MEAL INDOORS

- 2 teaspoons peanut oil

PACK IT UP
Three 1-gallon freezer bags, labeled

SWIMMING RAMA

MAKES 3 freezer meals, 4–6 servings each

I developed this make-ahead recipe after I noticed that an entrée by this name was a favorite restaurant choice of several of my girlfriends. This popular Thai dish is chicken in a spicy peanut and coconut milk sauce, served over fresh spinach and rice. — LA

1 Trim chicken as desired and cut into bite-size pieces.

2 In a large skillet, combine coconut milk, fish sauce, curry paste, and honey, and bring to a simmer over medium heat. Add chicken and cook until no longer pink, about 20 minutes. Stir in ground peanuts. Remove from heat and cool.

3 Divide cooled chicken and sauce evenly among freezer bags.

4 Seal and freeze. Food will stay at optimal quality for up to 3 months in freezer.

TO COOK ONE FREEZER MEAL

1 Completely thaw one freezer meal in refrigerator.

2 In a large skillet, bring chicken and sauce to a simmer over medium heat and cook until heated through. Do not boil.

3 To serve, place a handful of fresh spinach leaves on each plate. Top with a generous serving of chicken and sauce. Pass hot steamed rice at the table.

INGREDIENTS

- 6 pounds boneless, skinless chicken breast halves (about 12 halves)
- 3 (13.5-ounce) cans coconut milk
- ¼ cup fish sauce
- 2 tablespoons red curry paste
- 1 tablespoon honey
- 1½ cups dry-roasted unsalted peanuts, finely ground

ON HAND FOR COOKING EACH FREEZER MEAL

Fresh spinach leaves

Steamed rice

PACK IT UP
Three 1-gallon freezer bags, labeled

TEX-MEX
CHICKEN FINGERS

MAKES 3 freezer meals, about 12 fingers each

INGREDIENTS

- 6 pounds boneless, skinless chicken breast halves (about 12 halves)
- 4 eggs, lightly beaten
- 6 cups plain dry breadcrumbs
- 3 tablespoons ground cumin
- 3 tablespoons granulated garlic
- 2 tablespoons chili powder
- 1 tablespoon salt
- 1 tablespoon cayenne pepper

Don't let the cayenne scare you away from these tasty chicken fingers. They're great for lunch, dinner on the run, or as a party appetizer. Try dipping them in salsa ranch dressing or chipotle barbecue sauce. Or slice the cooked fingers and serve atop a salad or bowl with black beans and other ingredients. — KN

---

1 Trim chicken as desired. Cut each breast half lengthwise into three strips. Set aside.

2 Place eggs in a shallow dish.

3 In a large bowl, combine breadcrumbs, cumin, garlic, chili powder, salt, and cayenne.

4 Dip each piece of chicken first into egg and then into breadcrumb mixture. Place breaded chicken pieces onto one or more baking sheets. Cover with plastic wrap and freeze until solid.

5 Once chicken fingers are frozen, remove from baking sheets and divide evenly among freezer bags. Seal and return to freezer. Food will stay at optimal quality for up to 3 months in freezer.

PACK IT UP

Plastic wrap

Three 1-gallon freezer bags, labeled

TO COOK ONE FREEZER MEAL

1 Completely thaw one freezer meal in refrigerator.

2 Preheat oven to 350°F (180°C).

3 Bake chicken fingers on a greased baking sheet for 30 minutes, or until chicken pulls apart easily and is no longer pink in center of thickest portion.

CASHEW
CHICKEN STIR-FRY

MAKES 3 freezer meals, 4–6 servings each

Cashews are such a delicious addition to a dish. Cashews have a lower fat content than almonds, walnuts, pecans, and peanuts, and are packed with nutrients.

---

1 Cut chicken into bite-size pieces. Divide chicken evenly among three unlabeled 1-gallon freezer bags.

2 In a medium bowl, combine soy sauce, wine, and fish sauce. Divide marinade evenly over chicken. Into each chicken bag, measure 1 teaspoon garlic, ¾ teaspoon ginger, and ½ teaspoon pepper flakes. Seal and gently shake each bag to combine contents.

3 Put 1 cup cashews into each sandwich bag and seal.

4 Place a bag of chicken and a bag of cashews into each labeled 1-gallon bag. Seal and freeze. Food will stay at optimal quality for up to 3 months in freezer.

TO COOK ONE FREEZER MEAL

1 Completely thaw one freezer meal in refrigerator.

2 In a wok or large skillet, heat oil over medium-high heat. Stir-fry chicken and sauce until meat is cooked through, about 10 minutes. Remove chicken from pan.

3 Add vegetables and stir-fry until tender crisp, about 5 minutes. Return chicken to pan and stir to combine. Sprinkle with cashews and serve.

INGREDIENTS

6	pounds boneless chicken thighs, skin removed
¾	cup soy sauce
⅓	cup red wine or cooking sherry
1	tablespoon fish sauce
3	teaspoons minced garlic
2¼	teaspoons minced ginger
1½	teaspoons red pepper flakes
3	cups unsalted cashews, raw or roasted

ON HAND FOR COOKING EACH FREEZER MEAL

2	teaspoons sesame oil
½	pound assorted fresh vegetables, cut into 1-inch pieces

PACK IT UP

Six 1-gallon freezer bags; label 3

Three sandwich bags

WHERE CAN I FIND THE FISH SAUCE?

Fish sauce, a condiment used in Southeast Asian cuisine, adds depth to marinades and stir-fry sauces. Look for it in the Asian aisle at your supermarket. There you'll also find toasted sesame oil, hoisin sauce, mango chutney, coconut milk, and red curry paste, which are called for in several other recipes.

TEQUILA-LIME CHICKEN

MAKES 3 freezer meals, 4 servings each

INGREDIENTS

- 6 pounds boneless, skinless chicken breast halves (about 12 halves)
- ¾ cup soy sauce
- ½ cup bottled margarita mix
- 3 tablespoons tequila
- 3 tablespoons lime juice
- 1 tablespoon dry mustard
- 3 teaspoons minced garlic

The first time I tested this recipe on my family, my then six-year-old enjoyed the dish so much, she ate an entire breast half herself — and asked for seconds. It has since become a family favorite. Try using the leftover chicken in taco salads with the works: avocado, fresh cherry tomatoes, fresh salsa, and a sprinkling of Cotija cheese. — KN

1 Trim chicken as desired. Divide chicken evenly among freezer bags.

2 In a medium bowl, combine soy sauce, margarita mix, tequila, lime juice, and mustard. Divide marinade evenly over chicken. Into each bag, measure 1 teaspoon garlic.

3 Seal and gently shake each bag to combine contents. Freeze. Food will stay at optimal quality for up to 3 months in freezer.

TO COOK ONE FREEZER MEAL
Completely thaw one freezer meal in refrigerator. This entrée can be prepared outdoors on a grill or in the kitchen using your broiler.

For Outdoor Cooking

1 Prepare a medium-low fire in a gas or charcoal grill.

2 Grill chicken, turning every 5 minutes and basting frequently with marinade, for 30 minutes, or until an instant-read thermometer inserted into thickest part of chicken reads 165°F (74°C). Do not baste chicken during last 5 minutes of grilling. Discard remaining marinade.

For Indoor Cooking
Slice each breast in half horizontally, so that no piece is more than 1 inch thick. Arrange chicken slices on a greased broiler pan. Broil chicken 5 inches from broiler, turning frequently and basting, for 15 to 20 minutes, or until an instant-read thermometer inserted into thickest part of chicken reads 165°F (74°C). Do not baste chicken during last 5 minutes of grilling. Discard remaining marinade.

TEQUILA TIP

Large bottles of tequila can be costly. If this recipe is the only reason to have tequila on hand, look for the tiny 50-milliliter bottle at the liquor store. You'll find you have enough for this recipe with a few drops left over.

PACK IT UP

Three 1-gallon freezer bags, labeled

PEANUT SATAY

MAKES 3 freezer meals, 4–6 servings each

These kabobs make for a fun alternative to the usual fare, and they're easy to prepare year-round. If you plan to use disposable wooden skewers, remember to soak them in water before threading on the chicken. Whether grilled or broiled, the kabobs pair well with sticky white rice and steamed fresh vegetables.

1 Cut chicken into ½-inch strips. Divide chicken evenly among freezer bags.

2 In a medium bowl, combine peanut butter, juice concentrate, soy sauce, ginger, orange zest, and hot pepper sauce; divide evenly over chicken. Into each bag, measure about ¼ cup scallions.

3 Seal and gently shake each bag to distribute scallions. Freeze. Food will stay at optimal quality for up to 3 months in freezer.

TO COOK ONE FREEZER MEAL

Completely thaw one freezer meal in refrigerator. This entrée can be prepared outdoors on a grill or in the kitchen using your broiler.

For Outdoor Cooking

1 Prepare a medium-low fire in a gas or charcoal grill.

2 If using wooden skewers, soak them in water while chicken is thawing. Thread chicken pieces onto skewers. Grill until chicken pulls apart easily and is no longer pink in center of thickest portion. Discard remaining marinade.

For Indoor Cooking

Thread chicken pieces onto skewers. Arrange kabobs on a greased broiler pan. Broil chicken 5 inches from heat for 10 to 14 minutes, turning frequently, until chicken pulls apart easily and is no longer pink in center of thickest portion. Discard remaining marinade.

WHAT IS ZEST?

When a recipe calls for the zest of a citrus fruit, it's referring to the colorful part of the skin. Don't confuse the zest with the white pith part, between the fruit and zest, as pith can be quite bitter. To remove the zest, wash and dry the fruit. Then, using a zester or fine grater, gently shave the colorful, outermost part of the peel.

INGREDIENTS

- 6 pounds boneless chicken thighs, skin removed
- ¾ cup natural chunky peanut butter
- ½ cup orange juice concentrate, thawed
- ⅓ cup soy sauce
- 1 tablespoon minced ginger
- 2 teaspoons orange zest
- ½ teaspoon hot pepper sauce
- 5 scallions, chopped (about ¾ cup)

ON HAND FOR COOKING EACH FREEZER MEAL

- 8 (9-inch) wooden or metal skewers

PACK IT UP
Three 1-gallon freezer bags, labeled

HONEY-GLAZED
CHICKEN THIGHS

MAKES 3 freezer meals, 5 servings each

INGREDIENTS

1½ cups honey

¾ cup (1½ sticks) butter (do not substitute margarine)

½ cup prepared mustard

1 tablespoon curry powder

2 teaspoons salt

7 pounds bone-in chicken thighs, skin removed (about 16 pieces)

You'd be amazed that the simple ingredients in this dish can produce such a delicious meal. When I ask my children what they want for dinner, this is often their request. Sure to be a hit in your house, too, it goes straight from the freezer to the oven. Easy on the cook! — LA

1 In a medium saucepan, combine honey, butter, mustard, curry powder, and salt. Cook, stirring, over medium heat, until all ingredients dissolve into a smooth sauce, about 3 minutes. Cool.

2 While sauce is cooling, divide chicken evenly among freezer bags. Divide cooled sauce evenly over chicken.

3 Seal and freeze. Food will stay at optimal quality for up to 3 months in freezer.

TO COOK ONE FREEZER MEAL

1 Thaw one freezer meal in refrigerator just long enough to remove from freezer bag.

2 Preheat oven to 350°F (180°C).

3 Place frozen chicken in an ungreased baking dish. Bake for 45 minutes. Remove dish from oven and separate chicken pieces into a single layer, placing pieces meaty side down to keep them moist. Bake for 1½ hours longer, or until sauce has browned and is thick and sticky and an instant-read thermometer inserted into thickest part of chicken reads 165°F (74°C). Chicken will be thoroughly cooked but still moist from sauce.

PACK IT UP

Three 1-gallon freezer bags, labeled

FREEZE FIRST!

Most of our recipes are equally good whether they are cooked and eaten the same day they are prepared or frozen first. This recipe should be frozen and baked while still frozen to allow the sauce time to caramelize before the chicken is overdone.

ROYAL THAI THIGHS

MAKES 3 freezer meals, 5 servings each

INGREDIENTS

- 7 pounds bone-in chicken thighs, skin removed (about 16 pieces)
- 6 scallions, chopped (about ½ cup)
- ½ cup hoisin sauce
- ½ cup natural peanut butter
- 1 cup coconut milk
- ¼ cup lemon juice
- ¼ cup toasted sesame oil
- ¼ cup soy sauce
- 3 teaspoons minced garlic
- 3 teaspoons minced ginger
- 1½ teaspoons red pepper flakes (optional)

Most of us have a friend or two we can rely on to share their outstanding recipe finds. Two such friends for me are Debbie and Terry, sisters who are both excellent cooks. They have generously shared their best recipes with me over the years, and this is my version of one of those gems. — LA

1 Divide chicken evenly among freezer bags.

2 In a medium bowl. whisk together scallions, hoisin, peanut butter, coconut milk, lemon juice, sesame oil, and soy sauce. Divide sauce evenly over chicken. Into each bag, measure 1 teaspoon garlic and 1 teaspoon ginger. Add ½ teaspoon pepper flakes to each bag, if desired.

3 Seal and gently shake each bag to combine contents. Freeze. Food will stay at optimal quality for up to 3 months in freezer.

TO COOK ONE FREEZER MEAL

1 Completely thaw one freezer meal in refrigerator.

2 Preheat oven to 375°F (190°C).

3 Place chicken in a lightly greased baking dish. Bake, uncovered, for 45 minutes, or until an instant-read thermometer inserted into thickest part of chicken reads 165°F (74°C).

PACK IT UP

Three 1-gallon freezer bags, labeled

HEAT UNITS

Hot peppers can be classified according to their Scoville heat units. The range of heat among peppers is large, with green bell peppers having 0 heat units and habaneros registering a sizzling 300,000 units or more. Thai food lovers and other food adventurers can substitute a hotter pepper for the red pepper flakes (approximately 20,000 heat units) in this recipe. Traditional Thai peppers, also called Asian hot, Thai hot, or bird peppers, can measure up to 100,000 heat units.

TERIYAKI CHICKEN

MAKES 3 freezer meals, 5 servings each

The simple sauce for this dish is always a hit with kids. You can substitute chicken legs for the thighs in this recipe. Or if you prefer a stir-fry, marinate strips of chicken breast in the sauce, then stir-fry in a very hot pan with a little oil. — LA

1 Divide chicken evenly among freezer bags.

2 In a small bowl, combine soy sauce, sugar, vinegar, and oil, stirring until sugar is dissolved. Divide marinade evenly over chicken. Into each bag, measure 1 teaspoon garlic and 1 teaspoon ginger.

3 Seal and gently shake each bag to combine contents. Freeze. Food will stay at optimal quality for up to 3 months in freezer.

TO COOK ONE FREEZER MEAL

1 Completely thaw one freezer meal in refrigerator.

2 Preheat oven to 350°F (180°C).

3 Place chicken in an ungreased baking dish. Bake, uncovered, for 1 hour, or until an instant-read thermometer inserted into thickest part of chicken reads 165°F (74°C). Turn pieces once or twice during baking. The longer the cooking time, the thicker and stickier the sauce will be.

INGREDIENTS

- 7 pounds bone-in chicken thighs, skin removed (about 16 pieces)
- 1 cup soy sauce
- 1 cup firmly packed brown sugar
- ¼ cup red wine vinegar
- 1 tablespoon vegetable oil
- 3 teaspoons minced garlic
- 3 teaspoons minced ginger

> **PACK IT UP**
> *Three 1-gallon freezer bags, labeled*

ABOUT MIXING MARINADES

In this recipe and in many others in the book, we ask you to divide the marinade evenly over the meat in the bags. Then, in a second step, you measure other ingredients, such as minced garlic, directly into each bag. We have found that certain ingredients will either sink to the bottom or float on top of a thin marinade, resulting in uneven distribution when the mixture is poured into the bags of meat. After you have all the ingredients in each bag, seal it and gently shake to combine its contents.

BERRY-ROASTED CHICKEN

MAKES 2 freezer meals, 4-6 servings each

INGREDIENTS

2   whole chickens (8–
    10 pounds total weight)

2   cups berry-flavored vin-
    aigrette dressing (try our
    homemade version on
    page 208)

2   cups frozen mixed berries
    (12 ounces)

1   cup chopped onion
    (about 1 medium)

½   teaspoon salt

½   teaspoon black pepper

ON HAND FOR COOKING
EACH FREEZER MEAL

Fresh raspberries
(optional)

PACK IT UP
Two 1-gallon freezer bags, labeled

A roasted chicken is a simple way to add protein to a meal, and there is often enough left over to use in a wrap, a salad, or a soup the next day.

1 Remove neck and giblets from chicken cavities and discard. Pat chickens dry with paper towels.

2 Put one chicken into each freezer bag. Over each chicken, measure 1 cup vinaigrette, 1 cup berries, ½ cup onion, ¼ teaspoon salt, and ¼ teaspoon pepper.

3 Seal and gently shake each bag to combine contents. Freeze. Food will stay at optimal quality for up to 4 months in freezer.

TO COOK ONE FREEZER MEAL

1 Completely thaw one freezer meal in refrigerator.

2 Preheat oven to 325°F (170°C).

3 Place chicken, breast side up, in a greased baking dish and pour marinade into cavity. Roast for about 1½ hours, or until an instant-read thermometer inserted into a thigh reads 165°F (74°C). Garnish with fresh raspberries, if desired.

SWEET CHICKEN
TOSTADA FILLING

MAKES 5 freezer packages, 2¾ cups each

The sweet flavors in this dish are a twist on traditional Southwestern cooking. This versatile filling can be used on regular tostada shells, taco shells, or tortillas in place of ground beef or beans. You might also consider using it in our Cinco Layer Bake (page 59) and Sweet Chicken Tostada Crowns (page 60). — KN

1 Cook both chickens (see Two Cooking Methods for Whole Chickens, page 65). Cool and pull meat from bones. Discard skin and bones. Cut chicken into bite-size pieces. (A whole chicken will yield about 1 cup of meat per pound.)

2 In a large bowl, and using an electric mixer, beat together cream cheese and salsa. Stir in the chicken. Divide mixture evenly among freezer bags, about 3 scant cups of filling in each.

3 Seal and freeze. Food will stay at optimal quality for up to 2 months in freezer.

TO COOK ONE FREEZER PACKAGE

1 Completely thaw one freezer package in refrigerator.

2 In a large skillet, bring filling to a simmer over medium-low heat. Do not boil.

INGREDIENTS

- 2 whole chickens (8–10 pounds total weight)
- 3 (8-ounce) packages cream cheese, softened
- 3 cups prepared mango salsa

PACK IT UP
Five 1-quart freezer bags, labeled

CINCO-LAYER BAKE

MAKES 6–8 servings

You'll notice the ingredient list calls for Sweet Chicken Tostada Filling (page 57) and Chipotle-Roasted Tomato Sauce (page 188). Canned enchilada sauce works well, too, but we prefer it like this. Serve with a fresh green salad or fruit salad with jicama. — KN

1 Preheat oven to 375°F (190°C).

2 Lightly coat bottom of a 9-inch square baking dish with cooking spray. Cover bottom entirely with 4 tortilla halves, overlapping as necessary. Spread 1½ cups of tostada filling over tortillas. Next layer with ¾ cup beans, ½ cup tomato sauce, and 1 cup cheese. Repeat with a layer of tortillas and remaining filling, beans, and tomato sauce. Add remaining 4 tortilla halves and top with 1 cup cheese.

3 Cover with foil and bake for 45 to 60 minutes, or until an instant-read thermometer inserted into center of the casserole reads 165°F (74°C).

4 Garnish with fresh tomatoes, guacamole, or salsa, if desired.

PREP AHEAD

2¾ cups (1-quart bag) Sweet Chicken Tostada Filling (page 57), thawed

1 cup Chipotle Roasted-Tomato Sauce (page 188), thawed

INGREDIENTS

6 (10-inch) flour tortillas, cut in half

1½ cups black beans, rinsed and drained

2 cups shredded Mexican blend cheese

OPTIONAL TOPPINGS

Chopped tomatoes, guacamole, or salsa

JUST RIGHT

Some people like their enchiladas gooey, whereas others prefer them drier and crunchy. Some like more black beans, others prefer less. Whatever your preferences, feel free to adjust the ingredients to your taste.

SWEET CHICKEN
TOSTADA CROWNS

MAKES 4 servings

PREP AHEAD

> 2 cups Sweet Chicken Tostada Filling (page 57), warmed

INGREDIENTS

> 4 tostada crowns
>
> 2 cups black beans, rinsed and drained
>
> 6 cups shredded lettuce
>
> 2 cups cooked brown rice, cooled (about ⅔ cup uncooked)
>
> 1⅓ cups shredded Mexican blend cheese
>
> 8 tablespoons prepared salsa, or more to taste
>
> 1 mango, peeled and chopped

OPTIONAL TOPPINGS

> Salsa, guacamole, sliced black olives, chopped tomatoes, or chopped green or red bell peppers

Tostada crowns, sometimes called tostada bowls because of their shape, offer a fun way to present a meal. The filling here is sweet and mild, but you can turn up the heat by mixing in jalapeños. Served for Cinco de Mayo or another festive occasion, these are sure to please.
— KN

---

1 Place 1 tostada crown on each of four plates. Spread ½ cup chicken filling on bottom of each crown, then layer with ½ cup black beans, 1½ cups lettuce, ½ cup rice, ⅓ cup cheese, 2 tablespoons salsa, and one-quarter of mango pieces.

2 Pass additional toppings at the table, if desired.

MEDITERRANEAN
ROAST CHICKEN

MAKES 2 freezer meals, 4–6 servings each

Add a side dish of couscous with pine nuts and a simple cucumber and yogurt salad to round out this meal.

1 Zest rind of both lemons. Cut 1 lemon into thin slices.

2 Remove neck and giblets from chicken cavity and discard. Pat chickens dry with paper towels.

3 Place chickens, breast side up, on a work surface. Gently loosen breast skin by working your fingers between skin and meat. Slide lemon slices under breast skin of each chicken. Put one chicken into each freezer bag.

4 Divide lemon zest evenly over chickens. Juice remaining lemon. Remove seeds and divide juice evenly over chickens. Into each bag, measure ½ cup olives, 2 tablespoons capers, 1 tablespoon oil, 1 teaspoon garlic, ½ teaspoon pepper, and ¼ teaspoon salt.

5 Seal and gently shake each bag to combine contents. Freeze. Food will stay at optimal quality for up to 4 months in freezer.

TO COOK ONE FREEZER MEAL

1 Completely thaw one freezer meal in refrigerator.

2 Preheat oven to 325°F (170°C).

3 Place chicken, breast side up, in a greased baking dish. Surround chicken with olives, capers, and marinade. Add just enough water to cover bottom of baking dish. Roast for about 1½ hours, or until an instant-read thermometer inserted into a thigh reads 165°F (74°C).

INGREDIENTS

- 2   lemons
- 2   whole chickens (8–10 pounds total weight)
- 1   (16-ounce) container pitted Kalamata olives (about 1 cup), drained
- 4   tablespoons capers, rinsed and drained
- 2   tablespoons olive oil
- 2   teaspoons minced garlic
- 1   teaspoon black pepper
- ½   teaspoon salt

PACK IT UP
Two 1-gallon freezer bags, labeled

JUICING LEMONS

In his book What Einstein Told His Cook, *Robert Wolke recommends first rolling the fruit on the counter and then heating it for 20 to 30 seconds in the microwave. Try this method (but be careful, the lemon could get hot!) only if you're squeezing the fruit by hand. If using an electric juicer or reamer, don't bother. As Wolke notes, you won't get any extra juice out of the lemon by using his method, but it will make squeezing out the lemon juice easier.*

CHICKEN À LA KING

MAKES 4 freezer meals, 6 servings each

INGREDIENTS

- 2 whole chickens (8–10 pounds total weight)
- 1 cup (2 sticks) butter
- 1 pound fresh white mushrooms, cleaned and sliced
- 1 cup all-purpose flour
- 6 cups half-and-half or light cream
- 3 cups water
- 2 tablespoons chicken base
- 1 teaspoon black pepper
- 4 green bell peppers, cut into 1-inch pieces

I like to pull this recipe out when only comfort food will do. This versatile dish is equally tasty over mashed potatoes, rice, noodles, or biscuits. — LA

---

1 Cook both chickens (see Two Cooking Methods for Whole Chickens, page 65).

2 Cool and pull meat from bones. Discard skin and bones. Cut chicken into bite-size pieces. (A whole chicken will yield about 1 cup of meat per pound.) Divide chicken evenly among freezer bags.

3 In a large saucepan, melt butter over medium heat. Add mushrooms and cook, stirring, until soft. Add flour and cook, stirring, for 2 minutes. Mixture will be lumpy. Gradually add half-and-half, then water, stirring constantly until sauce thickens. Whisk to make a smooth sauce. Stir in chicken base and black pepper. Cool sauce.

4 Divide cooled sauce evenly over chicken. Divide bell peppers evenly among bags of chicken.

5 Seal and freeze. Food will stay at optimal quality for up to 2 months in freezer.

PACK IT UP

Four 1-gallon freezer bags, labeled

TO COOK ONE FREEZER MEAL

1 Completely thaw one freezer meal in refrigerator.

2 In a large skillet, simmer chicken and sauce over medium heat until warmed through. Do not boil.

MINI CHICKEN POT PIES

MAKES 5–6 freezer meals, 12 mini pot pies each

INGREDIENTS

- 2 whole chickens (8–10 pounds total weight)
- 4 tablespoons butter
- 2 cups sliced carrots (about 5 medium)
- ½ cup diced onion
- ⅔ cup all-purpose flour
- 2 tablespoons poultry seasoning
- 2 teaspoons salt
- 3 cups chicken juices, reserved from cooked chickens and cooled
- 3 cups half-and-half or light cream
- 1 (10-ounce) package frozen peas (about 2½ cups)

ON HAND FOR COOKING EACH FREEZER MEAL

- 12 slices sandwich bread, cut into 3½-inch circles

PACK IT UP
Six 1-quart freezer bags, labeled

Some grocery stores sell large fresh and frozen chicken pot pies. Individuals who are sensitive to salt may appreciate this alternative to store-bought versions. Kids will have fun using a cookie cutter to cut the bread circles. —KN

1 Cook both chickens (see Two Cooking Methods for Whole Chickens, page 65).

2 Cool and pull meat from bones. Discard skin and bones. Reserve 3 cups chicken juices. Cut chicken into bite-size pieces. (A whole chicken will yield about 1 cup of meat per pound.)

3 In a large stockpot, melt butter. Add carrots and cook, stirring, for 7 minutes. Add onion and cook, stirring, until vegetables are soft, about 3 minutes. Stir in flour, poultry seasoning, and salt. Gradually add reserved chicken juices and half-and-half; stir constantly until sauce thickens. Cool sauce.

4 Add chicken and peas to cooled sauce. Spoon 2½ cups of chicken filling into each freezer bag.

5 Seal and freeze. Food will stay at optimal quality for up to 2 months in freezer.

TO COOK ONE FREEZER MEAL

1 Completely thaw one freezer meal in refrigerator.

2 Preheat oven to 350°F (180°C).

3 Gently press bread rounds into a greased 12-cup regular muffin pan, so that bottoms and sides of cups are covered. Bread may not go all the way to top of each form. Toast bread in oven for 8 to 10 minutes, or to desired firmness and color.

4 While bread is toasting, in a medium saucepan, bring chicken filling to a simmer. Do not boil.

5 Remove toasted bread cups from muffin pan. Fill each bread cup with chicken filling and serve.

TWO COOKING METHODS FOR WHOLE CHICKENS

We recommend you use one of two methods for cooking two whole chickens at once — slow cooking or oven roasting. You will need a 6-quart slow cooker or an oven roasting pan with a lid (or a deep pan and some foil to cover). It makes no difference what the chickens look like when they are cooked since you will be pulling them apart, so if you have to turn them any which way to fit them in the slow cooker or you decide to roast them breast side down to retain moisture in the white meat, you may do so. Each of these cooking methods has its advantages. Slow cooking produces a more flavorful broth, while oven roasting is much faster.

Slow Cooking

Remove neck and giblets from chicken cavity and discard. Place both chickens in a 6-quart slow cooker with 1 cup water and 2 bay leaves; cook on low for 8 to 10 hours, or overnight, or until an instant-read thermometer inserted into the thickest part of the thigh reads 165°F (74°C). Drain and reserve juices. Discard bay leaves. Refrigerate juices. Cool chicken until it is no longer too hot to handle. Pull meat from bones and cut it into bite-size pieces. Discard skin and bones. Remove fat from the top of the reserved chicken juices. Use the broth to replace the broth or chicken base in any of the chicken recipes.

Oven Roasting

Remove neck and giblets from chicken cavity and discard. Place both chickens in a large roasting pan with 2 cups water and 2 bay leaves; bake, covered, at 350°F (180°C) for 2 hours, or until an instant-read thermometer inserted into the thickest part of the thigh reads 165°F (74°C). Drain and reserve juices. Discard bay leaves. Refrigerate juices. Cool chicken until it is no longer too hot to handle. Pull meat from bones and cut it into bite-size pieces. Discard skin and bones. Remove fat from the top of the reserved chicken juices. Use these juices to replace the broth or chicken base in any of the chicken recipes.

ENCHILADAS SUIZA STACK

MAKES 3 freezer meals, 6 servings each

INGREDIENTS

2   whole chickens (8–10 pounds total weight)

½   cup (1 stick) butter

2   cups chopped onion (about 2 medium)

½   cup all-purpose flour

4   cups chicken broth

2   (7-ounce) cans diced green chiles

2   cups sour cream

36 corn tortillas

4   cups shredded Monterey Jack cheese (about 16 ounces)

It's much faster and easier to layer enchilada ingredients. But if you prefer to roll them individually, soften each corn tortilla in the hot sauce to prevent it from tearing. — LA

1 Cook both chickens (see Two Cooking Methods for Whole Chickens, page 65).

2 Cool and pull meat from bones. Discard skin and bones. Cut chicken into bite-size pieces. (A whole chicken will yield about 1 cup of meat per pound.)

3 In a large saucepan, melt butter over medium heat. Add onion and cook, stirring, until golden brown, about 5 minutes. Add flour; stir into a paste. Cook, stirring, for 2 minutes. Gradually add broth; cook, stirring constantly, until the sauce has thickened, about 8 minutes. Remove from heat and stir in green chiles and sour cream.

4 Spread ½ cup sauce over bottom of each pan. Cover bottom of each pan with 4 corn tortillas, tearing them to fit in one layer. Divide half of chicken among each pan. Sprinkle ⅓ cup cheese in each pan. Top with ½ cup sauce. Repeat with 4 more corn tortillas, remaining chicken, ⅓ cup cheese, ½ cup sauce. Finish with 4 corn tortillas in each pan and divide remaining sauce and cheese among pans.

5 Wrap each dish entirely in plastic wrap. Top with foil, label, and freeze. Food will stay at optimal quality for up to 2 months in freezer.

TO COOK ONE FREEZER MEAL

1 Completely thaw one freezer meal in refrigerator.

2 Remove foil and plastic wrap from baking dish and replace foil.

3 Preheat oven to 350°F (180°C).

4 Bake, covered, for 25 minutes. Remove foil and bake for 5 to 10 minutes longer, or until sauce is bubbling.

PACK IT UP

Three 13- by 9-inch baking dishes

Plastic wrap

Aluminum foil

MULLIGATAWNY SOUP

MAKES 4 freezer meals, 6 servings each

The creaminess of this thick chicken soup comes from coconut milk. You can adapt this to be dairy-free by replacing the butter with coconut oil. Omit flour for a gluten-free version; the thinner broth is equally good. — LA

1 Cook both chickens (see Two Cooking Methods for Whole Chickens, page 65).

2 Cool chicken and pull meat from bones. Discard skin and bones. Cut chicken into bite-size pieces. (A whole chicken will yield about 1 cup of meat per pound.)

3 In a large pot, melt butter over medium heat. Add carrots, celery, and onion, and cook, stirring, until vegetables begin to soften, about 5 minutes. Add flour and curry powder; cook, stirring, for 5 minutes. Cool.

4 Divide vegetable mixture and chicken evenly among four unlabeled 1-gallon freezer bags.

5 Add 4 cups broth, 1 can coconut milk, and 1 teaspoon chicken base to each bag of vegetables and chicken. Seal.

6 Divide cooked rice evenly among each 1-quart bag. Seal. Place one bag of soup and one bag of rice into each labeled 1-gallon bag.

7 Seal and freeze. Food will stay at optimal quality for up to 3 months in freezer.

TO COOK ONE FREEZER MEAL

1 Completely thaw one freezer meal in refrigerator.

2 In a large saucepan, reheat soup over medium-low heat. Do not boil.

INGREDIENTS

- 2 whole chickens (8–10 pounds total)
- ½ cup (1 stick) butter
- 5 cups finely diced carrots (about 10 medium)
- 4 cups finely diced celery (about 8 large stalks)
- 4 cups finely diced onions (about 2 large)
- ½ cup all-purpose flour
- 2 tablespoons curry powder
- 16 cups (4 quarts) chicken broth
- 4 (13.5-ounce) cans coconut milk
- 4 teaspoons chicken base
- 8 cups cooked basmati rice, cooled (about 2⅔ cups, uncooked)

PACK IT UP

Eight 1-gallon freezer bags; label 4

Four 1-quart freezer bags

URBAN GARLIC CHICKEN

MAKES 2 freezer meals, 4–6 servings each

INGREDIENTS

- 2 whole chickens (8–10 pounds total weight)
- ¼ cup olive oil
- 2 tablespoons red wine vinegar
- 1 tablespoon minced garlic
- 1 tablespoon dried thyme
- 2 teaspoons salt
- 1 teaspoon black pepper
- 2 carrots, peeled and cut in half
- 2 celery stalks, cut in half
- 1 onion, peeled and cut in half

PACK IT UP

Two 1-gallon freezer bags, labeled

Two 1-quart freezer bags

I have my sister Shannon to thank for the name of this dish. During a telephone conversation one day, I said "herb and garlic," which she heard as "urban garlic." It stuck. — LA

1 Remove neck and giblets from chicken cavity and discard. Pat chickens dry with paper towels.

2 In a small bowl, combine oil, vinegar, garlic, thyme, salt, and pepper.

3 Place chickens, breast side up, on a work surface. Gently loosen skin on breast and legs by working your fingers between skin and meat. Using half of marinade for each chicken, rub under and over skin and in cavity. Put one chicken in each 1-gallon freezer bag.

4 Divide carrots, celery, and onion evenly between 1-quart freezer bags and seal. Place one bag of vegetables directly into each bag of chicken.

5 Seal and freeze. Food will stay at optimal quality for up to 4 months in freezer.

TO COOK ONE FREEZER MEAL

Oven

1 Completely thaw one freezer meal in refrigerator.

2 Preheat oven to 325°F (170°C).

3 Place chicken, breast side up, in a greased baking dish. Put carrot, celery, and onion in cavity. Roast for about 1½ hours, or until an instant-read thermometer inserted into a thigh reads 165°F (74°C).

Slow Cooker

1 Place frozen prepared chicken and vegetables in slow cooker. Do this only if you have a slow cooker with a removable insert. Cook on low for 8 to 10 hours. Drain juices, reserve, and cool.

2 Preheat oven to 350°F (180°C).

3 Place the uncovered crock in oven for 15 minutes to brown skin. Meanwhile, use reserved juices to make gravy or a sauce reduction.

CHICKEN WINGS

MAKES 3 freezer meals, 30 wings each

Who doesn't love a good chicken wing? These are the best! — LA

1 Turn on oven broiler.

2 On a rimmed baking sheet, spread wings in a single layer. You may want to line the sheet with foil for easier cleanup.

3 Brown wings under broiler, about 5 minutes each side. If wings are frozen, broil about 10 minutes on each side. Drain excess liquid from pan.

4 Meanwhile, in a medium pot, mix ketchup, honey, chili sauce, vinegar, water, onion, brown sugar, mustard, soy sauce, Worcestershire, and garlic, and simmer over low heat for 10 minutes.

5 Cool wings and sauce and divide evenly among freezer bags. Food will stay at optimal quality for up to 3 months in freezer.

TO COOK ONE BATCH OF WINGS
Wings can be cooked when frozen or thawed.

1 Preheat oven to 375°F (190°C).

2 Place wings in a single layer on a rimmed baking sheet. You may want to line the sheet with foil for easier cleanup.

3 Bake, uncovered, for about 40 minutes, or until sauce has thickened and is sticky and chicken is cooked through. Turn and baste wings with sauce in pan every 10 minutes.

INGREDIENTS

- 10 pounds chicken wings (about 90 pieces), fresh or frozen
- 2 cups ketchup
- 1 cup honey
- 1 cup sweet red chili sauce
- 1 cup red wine vinegar
- 1 cup water
- ½ cup minced onion
- ½ cup firmly packed brown sugar
- ¼ cup spicy brown mustard
- ¼ cup soy sauce
- ¼ cup Worcestershire sauce
- 1 tablespoon minced garlic

PACK IT UP
Three 1-gallon freezer bags, labeled

BEEF
MAIN DISHES

BEEF AND BEAN BURRITOS

MAKES 8 freezer meals, 5 servings each

INGREDIENTS

- 40 (10-inch) flour tortillas, uncooked preferred, such as Tortilla Land brand
- 6 pounds lean ground beef
- 1 cup taco seasoning (see page 148 for a homemade recipe)
- 3 cups water
- 8 (15-ounce) cans refried beans, any variety (see Homemade Refried Beans, below, for how to make your own)

PACK IT UP

Aluminum foil or parchment paper and plastic wrap

Eight 1-gallon freezer bags, labeled

We keep these on hand for quick lunches — homemade "fast food."
— LA

1 If you are using uncooked tortillas, cook them all according to package directions. Keep them warm in a clean, dry tea towel.

2 In a large stockpot, brown beef over medium heat until no longer pink, about 20 minutes. Drain and discard fat. Add taco seasoning. Stir in water and simmer mixture over medium heat until liquid is almost entirely evaporated, about 20 minutes. Cool.

3 Spread ¼ cup ground beef and ⅓ cup refried beans on each tortilla. Wrap burrito-style and then wrap each piece individually in foil or parchment paper and then in plastic wrap, depending on how you will reheat them. Divide packets evenly among freezer bags.

4 Seal and freeze. Food will stay at optimal quality for up to 3 months in freezer.

TO COOK ONE FREEZER MEAL

Thaw burritos in refrigerator or reheat them straight from freezer.
MICROWAVE (PARCHMENT WRAPPED). Remove plastic wrap, defrost, and reheat.
OVEN (FOIL WRAPPED). Bake in foil at 375°F (190°C) for 30 minutes if frozen, 300°F (150°C) for 20 minutes if thawed.

HOMEMADE LOW-FAT "REFRIED" BEANS

To make your own refried beans, begin with 2½ pounds (about 5 cups) of dried pinto beans. Put them in a large stockpot with plenty of water to cover. Bring the beans to a boil; boil for 2 minutes. Turn off the heat, cover the pot, and let the beans stand for 1 hour. Drain, rinse the beans, and return them to the pot. Add 15 cups water and simmer for 2 hours. Authentic refried beans are cooked with lard. I prefer to pulse the cooked beans to the desired consistency in my food processor and forgo the lard. Season the beans according to your preference — salt, pepper, garlic, cumin, and chili powder are nice choices.

CHEESY CHILADA BAKE

MAKES 4 freezer meals, 8 servings each

If ever there was a "football food," this qualifies. Straight from the oven next to the chips, salsa, and drinks: Touchdown! — KN

1 In a large stockpot, brown beef, bell peppers, onions, and garlic over medium heat until beef is no longer pink, about 30 minutes. Drain and discard fat. Stir in tomato sauce, beans, picante sauce, cumin, and salt.

2 Spread 4 cups meat mixture over bottom of each baking dish. Cover meat mixture with 6 corn tortillas, overlapping edges as necessary to fit in a single layer. Spread 1 cup cheese over tortillas. Repeat each layer, finishing with a cheese topping.

3 Wrap each dish entirely in plastic wrap. Top with foil, label, and freeze. Food will stay at optimal quality for up to 3 months in freezer.

TO COOK ONE FREEZER MEAL

1 Completely thaw one freezer meal in refrigerator.

2 Preheat oven to 350°F (180°C).

3 Remove foil and plastic wrap from baking dish and replace foil. Bake for 40 minutes, or until center is hot and edges are bubbly.

INGREDIENTS

- 6 pounds lean ground beef
- 4 green bell peppers, diced
- 4 medium onions, diced
- 2 teaspoons minced garlic
- 4 (15-ounce) cans tomato sauce
- 4 (14.5-ounce) cans pinto beans, drained and rinsed
- 4 cups picante sauce
- 2 teaspoons ground cumin
- 2 teaspoons salt
- 48 corn tortillas
- 8 cups shredded Mexican cheese blend (about 2 pounds)

> ### PACK IT UP
> *Four 13- by 9-inch baking dishes, greased*
>
> *Plastic wrap*
>
> *Aluminum foil*

FOIL PANS

In our recipes that call for freezing the food in baking dishes, reusable or disposable foil pans also work well. Plus, they're a perfect choice if you'll be sharing or giving meals away.

BEEF AND BOW TIE SOUP

MAKES 3 freezer meals, 6 servings each

This simple soup boasts big flavor and is family friendly. Cooking and freezing the pasta separately ensures very little prep at dinnertime. — LA

1 In a large skillet or pot, brown beef over medium heat until no longer pink, about 15 minutes. If beef is very lean, don't drain. Cool.

2 Divide beef evenly among three unlabeled 1-gallon freezer bags.

3 Into each bag of beef, measure 2 cups carrots, 1½ cups celery, 1 cup onion, 1 can tomato sauce, 1 can diced tomatoes, 1 teaspoon oregano, 1 teaspoon parsley, ½ teaspoon salt, and ¼ teaspoon pepper. Seal.

4 Divide cooked pasta among 1-quart freezer bags. Seal. Place one bag of soup and one bag of pasta into each labeled 1-gallon bag.

5 Seal and freeze. Food will stay at optimal quality for up to 4 months in freezer.

TO COOK ONE FREEZER MEAL

1 Place frozen or thawed soup into a slow cooker.

2 Add 4 cups water. Do not add cooked pasta yet.

3 Cook on low for 6 to 8 hours or on high for 3 to 4 hours.

4 Stir in pasta and heat through before serving. Serve with a sprinkle of Parmesan cheese, if desired.

INGREDIENTS

- 3 pounds ground beef
- 6 cups sliced carrots (about 12 medium)
- 4½ cups sliced celery (about 9 medium stalks)
- 3 cups chopped onion (about 3 small)
- 3 (15-ounce) cans tomato sauce
- 3 (14.5-ounce) cans diced tomatoes
- 3 teaspoons dried oregano
- 3 teaspoons dried parsley
- 1½ teaspoons salt
- ¾ teaspoon black pepper
- 6 cups cooked mini bow ties (farfalle) or other small pasta, cooled (one 1-pound box uncooked)

ON HAND FOR COOKING EACH FREEZER MEAL

- 4 cups water

  Parmesan cheese (optional)

PACK IT UP

Six 1-gallon freezer bags; label 3

Three 1-quart freezer bags

SPANISH RICE

MAKES 6 freezer meals, 6–8 servings each

INGREDIENTS

6 pounds lean ground beef

24 cups Basic Red Sauce (page 189)

12 cups cooked white or brown rice, cooled (about 4 cups, uncooked)

1 large onion, chopped

2 green bell peppers, chopped

3 (2¼-ounce) cans sliced black olives (about 1½ cups)

12 cups shredded cheddar cheese (about 3 pounds)

PACK IT UP
Twelve 1-gallon freezer bags; label 6

Six 1-quart freezer bags

I have an aunt who is so capable and efficient, she makes everything she does look easy. Once, when I was at her home with my daughters having them fitted for the bridesmaid dresses she was making, our visit extended into the dinner hour. She insisted we stay, though she hadn't planned on having four more mouths to feed. She had exactly what was needed for this recipe. I usually need the benefit of planning, so I adapted her recipe for my own method. This has become one of my favorites. — LA

1 In a large stockpot, brown beef over medium heat until no longer pink, about 20 minutes. Drain and discard fat. Cool beef. Divide evenly among six unlabeled 1-gallon freezer bags.

2 Into each bag of meat, measure 4 cups red sauce and 2 cups cooked rice. Divide onion, bell peppers, and olives evenly among bags of meat.

3 Seal bags and massage gently to distribute ingredients.

4 Divide cheese evenly among 1-quart freezer bags and seal. Place one bag of meat mixture and one bag of cheese into each labeled 1-gallon bag.

5 Seal and freeze. Food will stay at optimal quality for up to 3 months in freezer.

TO COOK ONE FREEZER MEAL

1 Completely thaw one freezer meal in refrigerator.

2 Preheat oven to 350°F (180°C).

3 Put meat mixture in an ungreased baking dish and sprinkle with cheese. Bake, covered, for 30 to 40 minutes, or until sauce is bubbling and cheese is melted.

CLASSIC LASAGNA
LARGE PAN

MAKES 2 freezer meals, 12 servings each

There is no need to boil noodles in advance and no need to buy more-expensive "oven-ready" noodles! I was a late convert to assembling lasagnas with regular uncooked noodles, but once I realized that I didn't have to boil dozens of noodles to make several lasagnas at once, I was hooked. Using plenty of red sauce and freezing the entrée first creates the perfect noodles. Lasagna has never been so easy! — LA

1 In a large bowl, combine cottage cheese, eggs, and 2 cups Parmesan.

2 Lay baking dishes before you and spread ½ cup red sauce in bottom of each.

3 Assemble both lasagnas at once in layers in the following order:

Layer 1
- 3 uncooked noodles
- 2 cups red sauce
- 1 cup cooked ground beef
- 1½ cups cottage cheese mixture
- 1 cup mozzarella

Layer 2
- 3 uncooked noodles
- 2 cups red sauce
- 1 cup cooked ground beef — or whatever remains
- 1½ cups cottage cheese mixture — or whatever remains
- 1 cup mozzarella

Layer 3
- 3 uncooked noodles
- 2 cups red sauce — or whatever remains
- 2 cups mozzarella
- ½ cup Parmesan

4 Wrap each dish entirely in plastic wrap. Top with foil, label, and freeze. Food will stay at optimal quality for up to 3 months in freezer.

TO COOK ONE FREEZER MEAL

1 Thaw one freezer meal in refrigerator or bake it straight from freezer.

2 Preheat oven to 375°F (190°C).

3 Remove foil and plastic wrap from baking dish and replace foil. Place dish on a rimmed baking sheet and bake for 1½ hours if thawed, 2 hours if frozen. Remove foil and continue baking for 20 minutes, or until lasagna is bubbling and cheese is browned. Remove from oven and let stand for 10 minutes before slicing and serving.

INGREDIENTS

- 1 (48-ounce) container cottage cheese (about 6 cups)
- 4 eggs, lightly beaten
- 3 cups shredded Parmesan cheese
- 13 cups Basic Red Sauce (page 189)
- 18 regular lasagna noodles, uncooked
- 2 pounds lean ground beef, cooked and drained
- 8 cups shredded mozzarella cheese (about 2 pounds)

PACK IT UP
Two 13- by 9- by 2-inch baking dishes (or deeper)

Plastic wrap

Aluminum foil

CLASSIC LASAGNA
SMALL PAN

MAKES 4 freezer meals, 4–6 servings each

These smaller lasagnas are the perfect size for smaller families. There is no need to use "no boil" or "oven-ready" noodles; the regular kind will cook up perfectly when assembled uncooked in the lasagna. — LA

1 In a large bowl, combine cottage cheese, eggs, and 2 cups Parmesan in a large bowl.

2 Lay baking dishes before you and spread ¼ cup red sauce in bottom of each.

3 Assemble all four lasagnas at once in layers in the following order:

INGREDIENTS

- 1 (48-ounce) container cottage cheese (about 6 cups)
- 4 eggs, lightly beaten
- 3 cups shredded Parmesan cheese
- 13 cups Basic Red Sauce (page 189)
- 24 regular lasagna noodles, uncooked
- 2 pounds lean ground beef, cooked and drained
- 8 cups shredded mozzarella cheese (about 2 pounds)

Layer 1
- 2 uncooked noodles
- 1 cup red sauce
- ½ cup cooked ground beef
- ¾ cup cottage cheese mixture
- ½ cup mozzarella

Layer 2
- 2 uncooked noodles
- 1 cup red sauce
- ½ cup cooked ground beef — or whatever remains
- ¾ cup cottage cheese mixture — or whatever remains
- ½ cup mozzarella

Layer 3
- 2 uncooked noodles
- 1 cup red sauce — or whatever remains
- 1 cup mozzarella
- ¼ cup Parmesan

4 Wrap each dish entirely in plastic wrap. Top with foil, label, and freeze. Food will stay at optimal quality for up to 3 months in freezer.

TO COOK ONE FREEZER MEAL

1 Thaw one freezer meal in refrigerator or bake it straight from freezer.

2 Preheat oven to 375°F (190°C).

3 Remove foil and plastic wrap from baking dish and replace foil. Bake for 1 hour if thawed, 1¼ hours if frozen. Remove foil and continue baking for 10 minutes, or until lasagna is bubbling and cheese is browned. Remove from oven and let stand for 10 minutes before slicing and serving.

PACK IT UP

Four 12½- by 6½- by 3-inch foil loaf pans (also known as 5-pound loaf pans or ⅓-size steam table pans)

Plastic wrap

Aluminum foil

HABANERO AND GREEN CHILE
HAMBURGERS

MAKES 4 freezer meals, 6 servings each

INGREDIENTS

12 habanero and green
    chile–flavored sausages,
    or other spicy sausages

6 pounds lean ground beef

Why not spice up those burgers with some gourmet seasoned sausages? Not only are these burgers tasty, but they're also a cinch to prepare — wonderful fare for a lazy summer evening. — KN

---

1 Remove and discard casings from sausage and crumble meat into a large bowl. Add beef and, using your hands, mix until well combined.

2 Divide meat into 24 equal portions; form into patties. Place patties in a single layer on a rimmed baking sheet. Cover baking sheet with plastic wrap and freeze for 1 hour.

3 Divide frozen patties evenly among freezer bags, separating layers with waxed paper. Discard plastic wrap. Seal and refreeze. Food will stay at optimal quality for up to 3 months in freezer.

PACK IT UP

Plastic wrap

Waxed paper

Four 1-gallon freezer bags, labeled

TO COOK ONE FREEZER MEAL

Prepare on an outdoor grill or indoors under a broiler.

1 Remove desired number of patties from freezer. Place on a plate and thaw completely in refrigerator.

For Outdoor Cooking

1 Prepare a medium-low fire on a gas or charcoal grill.

2 Cook burgers for 5 to 6 minutes per side, or until an instant-read thermometer inserted into thickest part of patty reads 160°F (71°C).

For Indoor Cooking

1 Arrange burgers on a broiler pan.

2 Broil patties under high heat for 5 minutes on each side, or until internal temperature reaches 160°F (71°C).

SAFE COOKING TEMPERATURES

One of the best ways to prevent food-borne illness is to make sure your hamburgers are thoroughly cooked, meeting temperature levels recommended by food safety experts. The internal temperature should reach 160°F (71°C).

MEXI-STUFFED PEPPERS

MAKES 4 freezer meals, 6 servings each

This dish takes a little extra time to prepare, but with its festive flavors and colors, it's worth it. Serve with sour cream, guacamole, or blue corn chips to highlight the peppers' intense red color. — KN

1 In a large stockpot, brown beef, onion, and garlic over medium heat until beef is no longer pink, about 30 minutes. Drain and discard fat. Cool beef. Stir in tomato sauce, corn, rice, and taco seasoning. Divide mixture evenly among freezer bags.

2 Seal and freeze. Food will stay at optimal quality for up to 3 months in freezer.

TO COOK ONE FREEZER MEAL

1 Completely thaw one freezer meal in refrigerator.

2 Preheat oven to 350°F (180°C).

3 Prepare peppers for stuffing: wash, cut off tops, and seed peppers. Fill each with meat mixture. Sprinkle with cheese. Place on a greased rimmed baking sheet. Bake for 35 minutes, or until filling is hot.

INGREDIENTS

- 6 pounds lean ground beef
- 2 cups diced onion (about 2 medium)
- ¼ cup minced garlic
- 4 (15-ounce) cans tomato sauce (8 cups)
- 4 cups frozen corn
- 4 cups cooked rice, cooled (about 1⅓ cups uncooked)
- 1 cup taco seasoning, such as Penzeys Bold Taco Seasoning or try my homemade version on page 148

ON HAND FOR COOKING EACH FREEZER MEAL

- 6 red bell peppers
- 1 cup shredded Mexican cheese blend

> **PACK IT UP**
> *Four 1-gallon freezer bags, labeled*

MAKE IT VEGETARIAN

Make a meatless variation of this dish by using a soybean substitute (such as MorningStar Farms or Boca meatless crumbles) in place of the beef. Instead of being added at the beginning, however, the beef substitute is added to the mixture just before stuffing the peppers. Make the sauce and freeze it as directed, omitting the ground beef. After the sauce has thawed, mix in 3 cups ground beef substitute. Fill each pepper and bake as directed.

MOROCCAN MEATBALLS

MAKES 5 freezer meals, 12 meatballs each

INGREDIENTS

- 6 pounds lean ground beef
- 2 cups diced red onion (about 2 medium)
- 1 cup packed fresh mint leaves, rinsed, then chopped fine
- 4 eggs
- 3 tablespoons minced garlic
- 2 cups wheat bran
- 3 tablespoons ground cumin
- 1 tablespoon ground coriander
- 1 tablespoon sugar
- 1 tablespoon salt (or more to taste)
- 1 teaspoon black pepper

ON HAND FOR COOKING EACH FREEZER MEAL

- 1–2 tablespoons olive oil

PACK IT UP

Five 1-gallon freezer bags, labeled

These flavorful meatballs contain a generous amount of fresh mint and spices common in North Africa. Consider serving with orzo pasta or couscous. — KN

1 In a large bowl, and using your hands, thoroughly combine beef, onion, mint, eggs, and garlic. Set aside.

2 In a medium bowl, combine wheat bran, cumin, coriander, sugar, salt, and pepper.

3 Add bran mixture to meat mixture and combine well.

4 Divide meat into five equal portions. Shape each portion into 12 oval meatballs, for a total of 60 meatballs.

5 Place meatballs in a single layer on a rimmed baking sheet. Cover baking sheet with plastic wrap and freeze for 1 hour.

6 Divide frozen meatballs evenly among freezer bags. Discard plastic wrap. Seal and return to freezer. Food will stay at optimal quality for up to 3 months in freezer.

TO COOK ONE FREEZER MEAL

1 Completely thaw one freezer meal in refrigerator.

2 Preheat oven to 450°F (230°C).

3 In an ovenproof skillet, heat oil over medium heat. Cook meatballs until browned on all sides, 8 to 10 minutes.

4 Place skillet in oven and bake for 10 to 15 minutes, or until an instant-read thermometer inserted into center of a meatball reads 160°F (71°C).

SWEET-AND-SOUR MEATBALLS

MAKES 6 freezer meals, about 20 meatballs each

These meatballs are perfect over rice or on their own as a potluck dish. If you want a few more veggies, add bite-size pieces of raw green bell pepper, onion, or carrot to the bags along with the pineapple tidbits before sealing and freezing. For guests who like a bit of zip, I offer chopped scallions and a little hot chili paste when I serve this dish. — LA

1 To make meatballs: Preheat oven to 500°F (260°C).

2 In a large bowl, and using your hands, thoroughly combine beef, breadcrumbs, milk, eggs, onion, garlic, salt, and pepper. Shape into 1- to 1½-inch meatballs, placing finished pieces close together on lightly greased broiler pans or rimmed baking sheets. Bake for 15 minutes, or until an instant-read thermometer inserted into center of a meatball reads 160°F (71°C). Cool meatballs.

3 To make sauce: Meanwhile, in a large stockpot, mix sugar and cornstarch. Add reserved pineapple juice, soy sauce, and vinegar; stir. Cook over medium heat, stirring occasionally, until sauce thickens, about 20 minutes. Cool sauce.

4 Divide cooled meatballs and sauce evenly among freezer bags. Divide drained pineapple tidbits evenly among bags of meatballs and sauce.

5 Seal and freeze. Food will stay at optimal quality for up to 3 months in freezer.

TO COOK ONE FREEZER MEAL
Completely thaw one freezer meal in refrigerator. Prepare in an oven or a slow cooker.

Oven
Preheat oven to 350°F (180°C). Put meatballs and sauce in an ungreased baking dish and bake, uncovered, for 30 minutes, or until meatballs are heated through.

Slow Cooker
Put meatballs and sauce in a slow cooker. Cook on low for 2 to 5 hours, or until meatballs are heated through.

MEATBALLS
- 6 pounds lean ground beef
- 3 cups dry breadcrumbs
- ⅔ cup milk
- 4 eggs, lightly beaten
- ¼ cup minced onion
- 2 tablespoons minced garlic
- 1 tablespoon salt
- 2 teaspoons black pepper

SAUCE
- 2 cups firmly packed brown sugar
- ½ cup cornstarch
- 1 (106-ounce) can pineapple tidbits, drained, juice reserved
- ½ cup soy sauce
- 2½ cups red wine vinegar

PACK IT UP
Six 1-gallon freezer bags, labeled

MOZZARELLA MEATBALLS

MAKES 6 freezer meals, about 20 meatballs each

MEATBALLS

15	pieces mozzarella string cheese or a 1-pound block of mozzarella cut into 120 cubes
6	pounds lean ground beef
3	cups dry breadcrumbs
⅔	cup milk
4	eggs, lightly beaten
¼	cup minced onion
2	tablespoons minced garlic
1	tablespoon salt
2	teaspoons black pepper

SAUCE

4	cups ketchup
2	cups firmly packed brown sugar
2	cups red wine vinegar
2	cups Worcestershire sauce
2	tablespoons minced garlic
2	tablespoons minced onion
1	tablespoon dry mustard
2	teaspoons black pepper

These delicious morsels drenched in a barbecue-style sauce have a surprise pocket of cheese inside. This all-star recipe is a favorite for many families. Serve over rice. — LA

1 To make meatballs: Remove string cheese from wrappers and cut each string into eight equal pieces. Place in a large bowl or 1-gallon freezer bag and freeze until it is time to form meatballs.

2 Preheat oven to 500°F (260°C).

3 In a large bowl, and using your hands, thoroughly combine beef, breadcrumbs, milk, eggs, onion, garlic, salt, and pepper. Shape into 1- to 1½-inch meatballs, each formed around a piece of frozen mozzarella. Seal meatballs well to keep cheese from oozing out.

4 Place meatballs close together on lightly greased broiler pans or rimmed baking sheets. Bake for 15 minutes, or until an instant-read thermometer inserted into center of a meatball reads 160°F (71°C). Cool meatballs.

5 To make sauce: Meanwhile, in a large bowl, mix ketchup, sugar, vinegar, Worcestershire, garlic, onion, mustard, and pepper. Divide sauce evenly among freezer bags. Divide cooled meatballs evenly among bags of sauce.

6 Seal and freeze. Food will stay at optimal quality for up to 3 months in freezer.

TO COOK ONE FREEZER MEAL

1 Completely thaw one freezer meal in refrigerator.

2 Preheat oven to 350°F (180°C).

3 Pour meatballs and sauce into an ungreased baking dish. Bake, uncovered, for 30 minutes, or until meatballs are heated through.

PACK IT UP

Six 1-gallon freezer bags, labeled

WHOLESALE CLUB BARGAINS

Ketchup can be had for two and a half times cheaper per ounce when purchased in the large bottles at the wholesale club versus the bottles at the grocery store. Use what you need in this and other recipes, and store the rest in a clean container with an airtight lid in the refrigerator. For serving, wash and reuse your grocery store ketchup bottles.

SALISBURY MEATBALLS

MAKES 6 freezer meals, about 20 meatballs each

I'm committed to cooking from scratch, so when I see a recipe that uses canned cream of mushroom soup, I simply make it myself. Homemade has better flavor, and when made ahead and frozen, it's just as quick to prepare for dinner as opening a can of soup. Serve meatballs over rice, mashed potatoes, or noodles. Note that when the entrée comes out of the freezer and is reheated, the sauce will be considerably thicker than it was before freezing.— LA

1 Preheat oven to 500°F (260°C).

2 To make meatballs: In a large bowl, and using your hands, thoroughly combine beef, breadcrumbs, milk, eggs, onion, garlic, salt, and pepper. Shape into 1- to 1½-inch meatballs, placing them close together on lightly greased broiler pans or rimmed baking sheets. Bake for 15 minutes, or until an instant-read thermometer inserted into center of a meatball reads 160°F (71°C). Cool meatballs.

3 To make sauce: Meanwhile, in a large stockpot, melt butter over medium heat. Add mushrooms and cook, stirring, until soft, about 7 minutes. Stir in flour. Mixture will be lumpy. Cook, stirring, for 2 minutes. Gradually stir in water and half-and-half, and cook, stirring, until sauce thickens, about 15 minutes. Whisk to make a smooth sauce. Add beef base, Worcestershire, and pepper; stir. Cool sauce.

4 Divide cooled meatballs and sauce evenly among freezer bags.

5 Seal and freeze. Food will stay at optimal quality for up to 2 months in freezer.

TO COOK ONE FREEZER MEAL

Completely thaw one freezer meal in refrigerator. Prepare on stove or in oven.

Stovetop

In a large skillet, bring meatballs and sauce to a simmer over medium heat until meatballs are heated through. Do not boil.

Oven

Preheat oven to 350°F (180°C). Pour meatballs and sauce into an ungreased baking dish and bake, uncovered, for 30 minutes, or until meatballs are heated through.

MEATBALLS

- 6 pounds lean ground beef
- 3 cups dry breadcrumbs
- ⅔ cup milk
- 4 eggs, lightly beaten
- ¼ cup minced onion
- 2 tablespoons minced garlic
- 1 tablespoon salt
- 2 teaspoons black pepper

SAUCE

- 1 cup (2 sticks) butter
- 1½ pounds fresh white mushrooms, cleaned and sliced
- 1 cup all-purpose flour
- 8 cups water
- 4 cups half-and-half or light cream
- 2 tablespoons beef base
- 2 tablespoons Worcestershire sauce
- 1½ teaspoons black pepper

> **PACK IT UP**
> *Six 1-gallon freezer bags, labeled*

TUSCAN MEATLOAF

MAKES 4 freezer meals, 4–5 servings each

I use a separate pair of insulated dish gloves when mixing large quantities of ground beef with my hands. When I'm finished mixing, I wash the gloves in hot, soapy water and allow them to dry thoroughly. Then I tuck them in a special place until next time. — KN

1 In a large bowl, and using your hands, thoroughly combine beef, cheese, breadcrumbs, pesto, onion, eggs, milk, tomatoes, Italian seasoning, and pepper.

2 Divide beef mixture into four equal parts. Press into loaf pans.

3 Cover each pan generously with plastic wrap, then foil. Label and freeze. Food will stay at optimal quality for up to 4 months in freezer.

TO COOK ONE FREEZER MEAL

1 Completely thaw one freezer meal in refrigerator.

2 Preheat oven to 350°F (180°C).

3 Remove foil and plastic wrap from baking dish and replace foil.

4 Bake for 1½ hours, or until a thermometer inserted into center reads 160°F (71°C). Remove foil during final 20 minutes of cooking and top meatloaf with marinara sauce.

INGREDIENTS

- 6 pounds lean ground beef
- 4 cups (about 12 ounces) shredded Pecorino Romano cheese
- 2 cups Italian-seasoned dry breadcrumbs
- 2 cups pesto
- 1½ cups diced onion (about 1 large)
- 4 eggs, lightly beaten
- 1 cup milk
- 1 cup chopped, drained oil-packed sun-dried tomatoes
- 2 tablespoons Italian seasoning spice blend
- 1 tablespoon black pepper

ON HAND FOR COOKING EACH FREEZER MEAL

- ½ cup marinara sauce

PACK IT UP

Four 9- by 5- by 3-inch loaf pans

Plastic wrap

Aluminum foil

CLASSIC CHILI

MAKES 4 freezer meals, 8 servings each

INGREDIENTS

- 6 pounds lean ground beef
- 4 cups chopped onion (about 4 medium)
- 1 tablespoon minced garlic
- 12 cups Basic Red Sauce (page 189)
- 8 (15-ounce) cans kidney beans (drained if you prefer)
- 4 (15-ounce) cans pork and beans
- 4 tablespoons chili powder
- 4 tablespoons hot pepper sauce
- 4 teaspoons dried oregano
- 4 teaspoons black pepper

This chili is always a huge hit. If you're cooking for people who are sensitive to spicy foods, serve the hot pepper sauce on the side. The resulting chili is still delicious. Offer toppings of shredded cheddar cheese, sour cream, chopped scallions, and sliced black olives. Serve cornbread or corn chips on the side. — LA

1 In a large stockpot, brown beef, onion, and garlic over medium heat until beef is no longer pink, about 30 minutes. Drain and discard fat. Cool beef; divide evenly among freezer bags.

2 Into each bag measure 3 cups red sauce, 2 cans kidney beans, 1 can pork and beans, 1 tablespoon chili powder, 1 tablespoon hot pepper sauce, 1 teaspoon oregano, and 1 teaspoon pepper.

3 Seal and freeze. Food will stay at optimal quality for up to 4 months in freezer.

TO COOK ONE FREEZER MEAL

1 Completely thaw one freezer meal in refrigerator.

2 In a medium saucepan, cook, stirring occasionally, over low heat until liquid cooks off and chili is thick, about 1 hour.

PACK IT UP

Four 1-gallon freezer bags, labeled

4 Bs FLANK STEAK

MAKES 2 freezer meals, 6 servings each

INGREDIENTS

- 2 flank steaks (about 1½ pounds each)
- 1½ cups Black Butte Porter or other dark beer
- ½ cup ketchup
- ¼ cup firmly packed dark brown sugar
- ¼ cup balsamic vinegar
- ¼ cup Dijon mustard
- 2 teaspoons minced garlic
- ½ teaspoon black pepper

PACK IT UP
Two 1-gallon freezer bags, labeled

This recipe is named for all the ingredients that start with the letter B. I greatly value the contribution of my local growers, producers, bakers, vintners, and brewers. If you live near a microbrewery, feel free to substitute their porter for the Oregon-brewed porter I use. If you don't have a local brewer, try a local mustard or make your own ketchup, or try a new balsamic vinegar — there's more than one way to incorporate local flavors into this recipe. Be adventurous. — KN

1 Trim steaks as desired. Put 1 steak in each freezer bag.

2 In a medium bowl, whisk together beer, ketchup, sugar, vinegar, and mustard. Divide marinade evenly over steaks. Into each bag, measure 1 teaspoon garlic and ¼ teaspoon pepper.

3 Seal and gently shake each bag to combine contents. Freeze. Food will stay at optimal quality for up to 3 months in freezer.

TO COOK ONE FREEZER MEAL

1 Completely thaw one freezer meal in refrigerator.

2 Prepare a medium fire in a gas or charcoal grill.

3 Grill steak for 15 to 20 minutes for medium-rare to medium (140–145°F/60–63°C). Turn occasionally and baste as desired. Do not baste during final 5 minutes of cooking. Discard remaining marinade.

BLACKJACK STEAK

MAKES 2 freezer meals, 6 servings each

Molasses is the inspiration for this recipe, and it imparts a distinct flavor that remains after cooking.

1 Trim steaks as desired. Put 1 steak in each freezer bag.

2 In a medium bowl, whisk together vinegar, molasses, thyme, salt, pepper, and nutmeg. Divide marinade evenly over steaks. Into each bag, measure 2 teaspoons garlic.

3 Seal and gently shake each bag to combine contents. Freeze. Food will stay at optimal quality for up to 3 months in freezer.

TO COOK ONE FREEZER MEAL

1 Completely thaw one freezer meal in refrigerator.

2 Prepare a medium fire in a gas or charcoal grill.

3 Grill steak for 15 to 20 minutes for medium-rare to medium (140–145°F/60–63°C). Turn occasionally and baste as desired. Do not baste during final 5 minutes of cooking. Discard remaining marinade.

INGREDIENTS

- 2 flank steaks (about 1½ pounds each)
- 1 cup balsamic vinegar
- 1 cup molasses
- 3 teaspoons dried thyme
- 1 teaspoon salt
- ½ teaspoon black pepper
- ½ teaspoon ground nutmeg
- 4 teaspoons minced garlic

PACK IT UP
Two 1-gallon freezer bags, labeled

ROSE CITY TERIYAKI

MAKES 2 freezer meals, 6 servings each

INGREDIENTS

- 2 flank steaks (about 1½ pounds each)
- ½ cup teriyaki sauce
- ½ cup toasted sesame oil
- ¼ cup orange juice
- 2 tablespoons soy sauce
- 2 teaspoons salt
- 1 cup chopped onion (about 1 medium)
- 1 tablespoon dried rosemary
- 2 teaspoons minced garlic
- ½ teaspoon red pepper flakes

PACK IT UP
Two 1-gallon freezer bags, labeled

Portland, Oregon, is called the Rose City. It and many other cities on the Pacific Rim in North America enjoy the culinary influence of their Asian neighbors. Often the flavors are Americanized or blended with other ethnic cuisines. The orange juice and rosemary in this teriyaki dish set it apart. — KN

1 Trim steaks as desired. Put 1 steak in each freezer bag.

2 In a medium bowl, whisk together teriyaki sauce, oil, orange juice, soy sauce, and salt. Divide marinade evenly over steaks. Into each bag, measure ½ cup onion, ½ tablespoon rosemary, 1 teaspoon garlic, and ¼ teaspoon pepper flakes.

3 Seal and gently shake each bag to combine contents. Freeze. Food will stay at optimal quality for up to 3 months in freezer.

TO COOK ONE FREEZER MEAL

1 Completely thaw one freezer meal in refrigerator.

2 Prepare a medium fire in a gas or charcoal grill.

3 Grill steak for 15 to 20 minutes for medium-rare to medium (140–145°F/60–63°C). Turn occasionally and baste as desired. Do not baste during final 5 minutes of cooking. Discard remaining marinade.

SESAME-SOY SIRLOIN

MAKES 3 freezer meals, 4 servings each

My children are not big meat eaters, so you can imagine my surprise when my two kids ate a third of a steak by themselves when they were preschoolers. Of all my recipes, this is their favorite. — KN

1 Divide steaks evenly among freezer bags.

2 In a medium bowl, whisk together soy sauce, lime juice, sugar, and oil until sugar dissolves. Divide marinade evenly over steaks. Into each bag, measure 1 tablespoon ginger, 1 tablespoon garlic, 1 tablespoon sesame seeds, 1 teaspoon red pepper flakes, and ¼ teaspoon black pepper.

3 Seal and gently shake each bag to combine contents. Freeze. Food will stay at optimal quality for up to 3 months in freezer.

TO COOK ONE FREEZER MEAL

1 Completely thaw one freezer meal in refrigerator.

2 Prepare a medium fire in a gas or charcoal grill.

3 Grill steak for 14 to 18 minutes for medium-rare to medium (140–145°F/60–63°C). Turn occasionally and baste as desired. Do not baste during final 5 minutes of cooking. Discard remaining marinade.

INGREDIENTS

- 3 boneless top sirloin steaks (about 2 pounds each)
- ½ cup soy sauce
- ¼ cup lime juice
- 2 tablespoons firmly packed brown sugar
- 2 tablespoons toasted sesame oil
- 3 tablespoons minced ginger
- 3 tablespoons minced garlic
- 3 tablespoons sesame seeds
- 3 teaspoons red pepper flakes
- ¾ teaspoon black pepper

PACK IT UP

Three 1-gallon freezer bags, labeled

BEEF FAJITAS

MAKES 4 freezer meals, 4 servings each

You'll know how good these fajitas are going to taste when you smell the marinade. It's out of this world! If you want to stretch this meal further, add refried beans to the stir-fried beef and vegetables and roll into burritos. — LA

1 Trim excess fat from steaks. Cutting across the grain, slice each steak into narrow strips. Divide beef evenly among four 1-gallon freezer bags.

2 In a medium bowl, whisk together lime juice, soy sauce, oil, chili powder, cumin, oregano, and black pepper. Divide marinade evenly over beef. Into each bag of beef strips, measure 2 teaspoons garlic. Seal and gently shake each bag to combine contents.

3 Divide onion and green pepper strips evenly among four 1-quart freezer bags. Seal. Measure 1 cup cheese into each remaining 1-quart bag. Seal. Put 10 tortillas into each remaining 1-gallon bag. Seal.

4 Into each 2-gallon freezer bag, place a bag of beef in marinade, a bag of onions and peppers, a bag of cheese, and a bag of tortillas.

5 Seal and freeze. Food will stay at optimal quality for up to 3 months in freezer.

TO COOK ONE FREEZER MEAL

1 Completely thaw one freezer meal in refrigerator.

2 In a large skillet, heat oil over medium-high heat. Add onions and peppers, and stir-fry until soft, about 3 minutes. Remove vegetables from skillet and add beef. Stir-fry beef until well browned, about 10 minutes. Remove pan from heat and return vegetables, stirring to combine. Warm tortillas and spoon beef and vegetables into the center of each. Add fajita toppings as desired.

JUMBO BAGS FOR BIG STORAGE JOBS

Two-gallon freezer bags are worth having for this recipe to keep everything together in one place in your freezer. If you can't find 2-gallon freezer bags, 2-gallon storage bags are an acceptable substitute. If you have no 2-gallon bags at all, wrap each complete freezer meal in a plastic grocery bag and clearly label. The outer bag can be reused.

INGREDIENTS

- 6 pounds boneless top sirloin steaks
- ½ cup lime juice
- ½ cup soy sauce
- ½ cup vegetable oil
- 2 teaspoons chili powder
- 2 teaspoons ground cumin
- 2 teaspoons dried oregano
- 1 teaspoon black pepper
- 8 teaspoons minced garlic (about 24 cloves)
- 4 large onion, cut into strips
- 4 large green bell peppers, cut into strips
- 4 cups shredded cheddar cheese (about 1 pound)
- 40 8-inch or 10-inch flour tortillas

ON HAND FOR COOKING EACH FREEZER MEAL

- 2 teaspoons vegetable oil

  Sour cream, salsa, guacamole, or other fajita toppings

SHANGHAI STIR-FRY

MAKES 3 freezer meals, 6 servings each

INGREDIENTS

- 6 pounds boneless top sirloin steaks
- ⅔ cup cranberry juice
- ½ cup soy sauce
- ½ cup firmly packed brown sugar
- 3 teaspoons minced garlic
- 3 teaspoons minced ginger
- 1½ teaspoons red pepper flakes

  Zest of 1 orange

ON HAND FOR COOKING EACH FREEZER MEAL

- 2 teaspoons vegetable oil
- 1 (11-ounce) can mandarin orange slices, drained
- 2 teaspoons sesame seeds

PACK IT UP
Three 1-gallon freezer bags, labeled

The flavor of sesame, the tang of cranberry, and the sweet surprise of mandarin orange make this stir-fry special. It is delicious served over your favorite rice.

1 Trim excess fat from steaks. Cutting across grain, slice each steak into narrow strips. Divide beef evenly among freezer bags.

2 In a medium bowl, whisk together cranberry juice, soy sauce, and sugar. Divide marinade evenly over beef. Into each bag, measure 1 teaspoon garlic, 1 teaspoon ginger, and ½ teaspoon pepper flakes. Divide orange zest evenly among bags.

3 Seal and gently shake each bag to combine contents. Freeze. Food will stay at optimal quality for up to 3 months in freezer.

TO COOK ONE FREEZER MEAL

1 Completely thaw one freezer meal in refrigerator.

2 Pour off marinade and reserve. In a large skillet, heat oil over medium-high heat. Add beef and stir-fry until well browned, about 10 minutes. Remove beef from pan and keep warm. Add marinade to skillet, reduce heat, and simmer for 3 minutes. Return beef to pan. Add oranges and stir to coat. Sprinkle with sesame seeds.

STEAK SKEWERS
WITH BLUE CHEESE DIPPING SAUCE

MAKES 3 freezer meals, 4 servings each

INGREDIENTS

- 6 pounds boneless top sirloin steaks
- ½ cup olive oil
- ¼ cup red wine vinegar
- 1½ teaspoons black pepper

SAUCE

- 1 (4–5-ounce) container crumbled blue cheese (about ¾ cup)
- 3 cups heavy cream
- ¾ teaspoon black pepper

ON HAND FOR COOKING EACH FREEZER MEAL

- 8 (9-inch) wooden or metal skewers

PACK IT UP

Six 1-gallon freezer bags; label 3

Three 1-quart freezer bags

If you love blue cheese and want to skip the steak, the sauce is also tasty over pasta. — LA

1 Trim excess fat from steaks. Cut into 1-inch cubes. Divide beef evenly among three unlabeled 1-gallon freezer bags.

2 In a small bowl, whisk together oil and vinegar. Divide marinade evenly over beef. Into each bag, measure ½ teaspoon pepper. Seal and gently shake each bag to combine contents.

3 To make sauce: Divide blue cheese among three 1-quart freezer bags. Into each bag of cheese, measure 1 cup heavy cream and ¼ teaspoon pepper. Seal bags.

4 Into each labeled 1-gallon freezer bag, place one bag of beef and one bag of sauce.

5 Seal and freeze. Food will stay at optimal quality for up to 2 months in freezer.

TO COOK ONE FREEZER MEAL

Prepare on an outdoor grill or indoors under a broiler.

1 Completely thaw one freezer meal in refrigerator.

For Outdoor Cooking

1 Prepare a medium fire in a gas or charcoal grill.

2 If using wooden skewers, soak them in water while beef is thawing. Thread steak pieces onto skewers. Grill, turning occasionally, for about 10 minutes, or until beef is done to your liking. Discard remaining marinade.

3 Meanwhile, in a small saucepan, heat blue cheese mixture over medium heat. Simmer gently, stirring frequently, until cream reduces and thickens into a velvety sauce. Serve as a dipping sauce with steak skewers.

For Indoor Cooking

1 Prepare skewers as in step 2, above. Arrange skewers on an ungreased broiler pan. Broil steak under high heat, 5 inches from heat source, turning frequently for about 10 minutes, or until beef is done to your liking. Discard remaining marinade.

2 Heat and serve cheese sauce as described in step 3, above.

BEEF-BARLEY SOUP

MAKES 4 freezer meals, 6–8 servings each

I think the secret to this delicious soup is our Basic Red Sauce. — LA

1 Trim beef as desired. Cut into bite-size pieces. Divide beef evenly among four unlabeled 1-gallon freezer bags.

2 Into each bag of beef, measure 1½ cups carrots, 1½ cups celery, 1 cup onion, one-fourth of bell peppers, 1 can tomatoes with juice, 1 cup red sauce, 1 tablespoon beef base, 1 teaspoon salt, ½ teaspoon black pepper. Seal.

3 Into each 1-quart freezer bag, measure ½ cup barley. Seal. Place one bag of soup and one bag of barley in each labeled 1-gallon bag.

4 Seal and freeze. Food will stay at optimal quality for up to 4 months in freezer.

TO COOK ONE FREEZER MEAL

1 Put frozen soup into a slow cooker. (Soup doesn't need to be thawed.)

2 Add 4 cups water and 1-quart bag of barley.

3 Cook until meat and vegetables are tender, 8 to 10 hours on low or 4 to 5 hours on high.

INGREDIENTS

- 6 pounds sirloin tip beef or other beef suitable for slow cooking
- 6 cups sliced carrots (about 12 medium)
- 6 cups sliced celery (about 12 stalks)
- 4 cups chopped onion (about 4 medium)
- 2 large green bell peppers, cut into 1-inch pieces
- 4 (14.5-ounce cans) diced tomatoes with juice (about 8 cups)
- 4 cups Basic Red Sauce (page 190)
- 4 tablespoons beef base
- 4 teaspoons salt
- 2 teaspoons black pepper
- 2 cups pearl barley (1-pound bag)

ON HAND FOR COOKING EACH FREEZER MEAL

- 4 cups water

PACK IT UP

Eight 1-gallon freezer bags; label 4

Four 1-quart freezer bags

GINGER BEEF

This beef dish has a subtle flavor, suitable for everyone. Serve over jasmine rice and top with fresh scallion or cilantro and toasted sesame seeds. — LA

1 Trim beef as desired. Cut into thick strips, about 2 by 5 inches. (The beef should not be in bite-size pieces.) Divide beef evenly among freezer bags.

2 Into each bag, measure 1 cup water, ½ cup scallions, ¼ cup soy sauce, 2 teaspoons beef base, 2 teaspoons garlic, and 2 teaspoons ginger.

3 Seal and freeze. Food will stay at optimal quality for up to 3 months in freezer.

TO COOK ONE FREEZER MEAL

1 Thaw one freezer meal in refrigerator or cook it straight from freezer.

2 Put beef and broth into a slow cooker. Cook on low until beef is fork-tender, 5 to 6 hours.

INGREDIENTS

- 6 pounds sirloin tip beef or other beef suitable for slow cooking
- 3 cups water
- 9 scallions, chopped (about 1½ cups)
- ¾ cup soy sauce
- 6 teaspoons beef base
- 6 teaspoons minced garlic
- 6 teaspoons minced ginger

PACK IT UP
Three 1-gallon freezer bags, labeled

BUYING TIPS

Packages of sirloin tip beef can vary in size by several pounds. Buy as close to 6 pounds as possible or, alternatively, in multiples of 3 pounds, and adjust the recipe accordingly. Because you're measuring ingredients into each bag separately, you can easily alter the number of freezer meals you make.

CHEESE STEAKS

MAKES 3 freezer meals, 6 servings each

INGREDIENTS

- 6 pounds sirloin tip beef or other beef suitable for slow cooking
- 3 cups water
- 6 teaspoons beef base
- 3 large green bell peppers, cut into strips
- 3 large onions, cut into strips
- 18 slices deli cheese (cheddar, Monterey Jack, or Swiss)
- 18 long bread rolls

ON HAND FOR COOKING EACH FREEZER MEAL

- 2 teaspoons vegetable oil

  Aluminum foil

PACK IT UP

Three 1-gallon freezer bags

Three 1-quart freezer bags

Plastic wrap

Three 2-gallon freezer bags, labeled

There is nothing quite as satisfying as a hot sandwich. For a flavor booster, try spreading some horseradish mayonnaise on the rolls before adding the beef. — LA

1 Trim beef as desired. Cut beef into three equal pieces. Place a piece of beef into each 1-gallon freezer bag. Into each bag, measure 1 cup water and 2 teaspoons beef base. Seal bags.

2 Divide bell peppers and onions evenly among 1-quart freezer bags. Seal.

3 Divide cheese into three portions of 6 slices each; enclose in plastic wrap. Divide rolls into three portions of 6 each; enclose in plastic wrap.

4 Place a bag of beef, a bag of peppers and onions, a stack of cheese slices, and a packet of rolls inside each 2-gallon freezer bag.

5 Seal and freeze. Food will stay at optimal quality for up to 3 months in freezer.

TO COOK ONE FREEZER MEAL

1 Thaw one freezer meal in refrigerator or cook it straight from freezer.

2 Put beef and broth into a slow cooker. Cook on low until the beef is tender and pulls apart easily with a fork, 5 to 6 hours. Remove beef from broth and set aside until cool enough to shred. Reserve broth.

3 Preheat oven to 350°F (180°C).

4 Meanwhile, in a large skillet, heat oil over medium-high heat. Add peppers and onions, and stir-fry until soft, about 3 minutes. Remove pan from heat. Slice and open rolls. Divide beef and vegetables evenly among rolls. Place a slice of cheese inside each sandwich; close and wrap in foil. Heat in oven for 10 minutes. Unwrap carefully. Serve with broth for dipping.

PORK
MAIN DISHES

4 Bs GRILLED CHOPS

MAKES 2 freezer meals, 6 servings each

INGREDIENTS

- 12 pork loin chops, boneless or bone-in (6–8 pounds)
- 1½ cups pale ale or other light beer
- ½ cup ketchup
- ¼ cup firmly packed brown sugar
- ¼ cup white balsamic vinegar
- ¼ cup Dijon mustard
- 2 teaspoons minced garlic
- ½ teaspoon black pepper

On vacation to the Oregon coast one summer, I happened upon a beer sale at a local microbrewery. I modified the 4 Bs Flank Steak recipe (page 94) for a pork dish to use up one of the lighter ales I liked least. The dish turned out quite good. — KN

1 Trim chops as desired. Divide chops evenly between freezer bags.

2 In a medium bowl, whisk together beer, ketchup, sugar, vinegar, and mustard. Divide marinade evenly over chops.

3 Into each bag, measure 1 teaspoon garlic and ¼ teaspoon pepper.

4 Seal and gently shake each bag to combine contents. Freeze. Food will stay at optimal quality for up to 3 months in freezer.

TO COOK ONE FREEZER MEAL

1 Completely thaw one freezer meal in refrigerator.

2 Prepare a medium-low fire in a gas or charcoal grill.

3 Grill chops for 10 to 15 minutes, or until an instant-read thermometer inserted into thickest part of a chop reads 145°F (63°C). Discard remaining marinade.

BALSAMIC VINEGAR

We have found that oftentimes balsamic vinegar is one of the rare ingredients that offer no substantial savings when purchased in bulk versus the grocery store. Since prices are comparable between the two, choose your favorite brand at either location. If you use a lot of balsamic vinegar, you may want to purchase larger bottles simply for the convenience of the size.

PEPPER JELLY PORK CHOPS

MAKES 3 freezer meals, 4 servings each

Look for this jelly at the farm stand or farmers' market, or in either the specialty aisle or near the peanut butter and preserves in a grocery store. Sweet with just a little kick, it adds a bit of fun to everyday pork chops.

1 Divide chops evenly among freezer bags.

2 In a medium bowl, whisk together jelly, mustard, vinegar, oil, and thyme. Divide marinade evenly over chops.

3 Seal and gently shake each bag to combine contents. Food will stay at optimal quality for up to 3 months in freezer.

TO COOK ONE FREEZER MEAL

Completely thaw one freezer meal in refrigerator. Prepare on an outdoor grill or indoors under a broiler.

For Outdoor Cooking

1 Prepare a medium fire in a gas or charcoal grill.

2 Grill chops, turning occasionally, for 10 to 15 minutes, or until an instant-read thermometer inserted into thickest part of a chop reads 145°F (63°C). Baste chops as desired. Do not baste during final 5 minutes of cooking. Discard remaining marinade.

For Indoor Cooking

Arrange chops on a greased broiler pan. Broil chops under high heat 5 inches from heat source, turning frequently, for 15 to 18 minutes, or until an instant-read thermometer inserted into thickest part of a chop reads 145°F (63°C). Baste chops as desired. Do not baste during final 5 minutes of cooking. Discard remaining marinade.

INGREDIENTS

- 12 pork loin chops, boneless or bone-in (6–8 pounds)
- 1 cup jalapeño pepper jelly
- 2 tablespoons spicy brown mustard
- 2 tablespoons balsamic vinegar
- 2 tablespoons olive oil
- 1½ teaspoons dried thyme

PACK IT UP
Three 1-gallon freezer bags, labeled

AN'S PORK CHOPS

MAKES 3 freezer meals, 4 servings each

INGREDIENTS

12	pork loin chops, boneless or bone-in (6–8 pounds)
1⅓	cups soy sauce
⅔	cup rice vinegar
½	cup sugar
¼	cup toasted sesame oil
3	tablespoons minced garlic
3	tablespoons minced ginger
¾	teaspoon cayenne pepper

I named this recipe after a local bento shop owner I used to know. She and her son always served the most wonderful food with such great hospitality. I still recall An's wide, warm smile, greeting us each time we ate there. This dish is sure to put a smile on your dinner guests' faces, too. Serve with steamed vegetables or Asian greens. — KN

1 Divide chops evenly among freezer bags.

2 In a medium bowl, whisk together soy sauce, vinegar, sugar, and oil. Divide marinade evenly over chops.

3 Into each bag, measure 1 tablespoon garlic, 1 tablespoon ginger, and ¼ teaspoon cayenne.

4 Seal and gently shake each bag to combine contents. Freeze. Food will stay at optimal quality for up to 3 months in freezer.

TO COOK ONE FREEZER MEAL

1 Completely thaw one freezer meal in refrigerator.

2 Prepare a medium-low fire in a gas or charcoal grill.

3 Grill chops for 10 to 15 minutes, or until an instant-read thermometer inserted into thickest part of a chop reads 145°F (63°C). Discard remaining marinade.

PACK IT UP

Three 1-gallon freezer bags, labeled

RICE VINEGAR

If you don't find rice vinegar (also called rice wine vinegar) among the other vinegars, try looking in the Asian food section of your grocery store. The strength of flavor among rice vinegars varies widely. If you find the flavors in this dish are unbalanced or have too heavy a vinegar taste, make a note to use less vinegar next time.

BASIL-BALSAMIC CHOPS

MAKES 3 freezer meals, 4 servings each

The marinade in this recipe is also our best-loved salad dressing. Make an extra batch to serve over salad greens — you may never buy commercial dressing again. You may substitute 6 pounds boneless, skinless chicken breast halves for the pork chops and grill until an instant-read thermometer inserted in the thickest part of the chicken reads 165°F (74°C). — LA

1 Divide chops evenly among freezer bags.

2 In a medium bowl, whisk together olive oil, vinegar, lemon juice, soy sauce, and honey. Divide marinade evenly over chops.

3 Into each bag, measure 1 teaspoon basil, 1 teaspoon garlic, and ¾ teaspoon pepper.

4 Seal and gently shake each bag to combine contents. Freeze. Food will stay at optimal quality for up to 3 months in freezer.

TO COOK ONE FREEZER MEAL
Completely thaw one freezer meal in refrigerator. Prepare on an outdoor grill or indoors under a broiler.

For Outdoor Cooking
1 Prepare a medium fire in a gas or charcoal grill.

2 Grill chops, turning occasionally, for 10 to 15 minutes, or until an instant-read thermometer inserted into thickest part of a chop reads 145°F (63°C). Discard remaining marinade.

For Indoor Cooking
Arrange chops on an ungreased broiler pan. Broil chops under high heat, 5 inches from heat source, turning frequently, for 15 to 18 minutes, or until an instant-read thermometer inserted into thickest part of a chop reads 145°F (63°C). Discard remaining marinade.

INGREDIENTS

12	pork loin chops, boneless or bone-in (6–8 pounds)
1	cup olive oil
½	cup balsamic vinegar
¼	cup lemon juice
¼	cup soy sauce
2	tablespoons honey
3	teaspoons dried basil
3	teaspoons minced garlic
2¼	teaspoons black pepper

PACK IT UP
Three 1-gallon freezer bags, labeled

CREATIVE LEFTOVERS

Leftover pork from this recipe is easily transformed into Basil-Balsamic Wraps: In a medium skillet, stir-fry leftover rice and bite-size pieces of pork over medium-high heat until heated through. Wrap in a flour tortilla and add shredded cheddar cheese, black beans, chopped scallion, and sour cream. Who says leftovers have to be boring!?

CAJUN BRAISED
SKILLET CHOPS

MAKES 2 freezer meals, 6 servings each

INGREDIENTS

12	pork loin chops, boneless or bone-in (6–8 pounds)
3	egg whites, lightly beaten
1	cup grated Parmesan cheese (about 3½ ounces)
2	tablespoons black pepper
2	tablespoons Cajun seasoning
1⅓	cups chicken broth
1	(15-ounce) can sweet corn, drained
1	(14.5-ounce) can petite-cut tomatoes
⅔	cup diced onion (about 1 small)
2	tablespoons minced garlic

ON HAND FOR COOKING EACH FREEZER MEAL

1½	tablespoons vegetable oil

PACK IT UP

Two 1-quart freezer bags

Two 1-gallon freezer bags, labeled

Here's a dish that's simply delicious! You'll find many Cajun spice blends at your local grocery store and online. I make a Tex-Mex variation of this dish: Simply substitute in equal measures bold taco seasoning (page 148) for the Cajun seasoning, Chipotle–Roasted Tomato Sauce (page 188) for the canned tomatoes, and Green Giant Mexicorn in place of plain corn. — KN

---

1 Trim chops as desired.

2 Lay out two shallow dishes. Put egg whites in one dish. In second dish, combine Parmesan, pepper, and Cajun seasoning. Dip chops into egg, then dredge in Parmesan coating.

3 Place each chop on a rimmed baking sheet. When all chops are coated, place pan in freezer for 1 hour. Discard remaining egg and Parmesan mixture.

4 Into each 1-quart freezer bag, measure ⅔ cup chicken broth, ⅔ cup corn, ⅔ cup tomatoes, ⅓ cup onion, and 1 tablespoon garlic. Seal.

5 Divide frozen chops evenly among 1-gallon freezer bags. Place one bag tomato mixture into each bag of chops.

6 Seal and freeze. Food will stay at optimal quality for up to 3 months in freezer.

TO COOK ONE FREEZER MEAL

1 Completely thaw one freezer meal in refrigerator.

2 In a deep skillet or Dutch oven, heat oil over medium heat. Fry chops 3 minutes on each side; remove from pan.

3 Pour broth and vegetables into pan. Gently scrape browned bits from bottom; reduce heat to medium-low. Return chops to pan. Simmer, covered, turning chops occasionally, until an instant-read thermometer inserted into thickest part of a chop reads 145°F (63°C), 15 to 20 minutes.

MUSTARD-OREGANO CHOPS

MAKES 3 freezer meals, 4 servings each

This beautiful yellow marinade mellows once grilled, leaving just the right amount of flavor and a golden color. — LA

1 Divide chops evenly among freezer bags.

2 In a medium bowl, whisk together mustard, lemon juice, vinegar, oil, and honey. Divide marinade evenly over chops. Into each bag, measure 1 teaspoon garlic and 1 teaspoon oregano.

3 Seal and gently shake each bag to combine contents. Freeze. Food will stay at optimal quality for up to 3 months in freezer.

TO COOK ONE FREEZER MEAL
Completely thaw one freezer meal in refrigerator. Prepare on an outdoor grill or indoors under a broiler.

For Outdoor Cooking

1 Prepare a medium fire in a gas or charcoal grill.

2 Grill chops, turning occasionally, for 10 to 15 minutes, or until an instant-read thermometer inserted into thickest part of a chop reads 145°F (63°C). Baste chops as desired. Do not baste during final 5 minutes of cooking. Discard remaining marinade.

For Indoor Cooking
Arrange chops on a greased broiler pan. Broil chops under high heat 5 inches from heat source, turning frequently, for 15 to 18 minutes, or until an instant-read thermometer inserted into the thickest part of a chop reads 145°F (63°C). Baste chops as desired. Do not baste during final 5 minutes of cooking. Discard remaining marinade.

RED WINE VINEGAR

Sales on vinegar can range from 10 to 25 percent off the everyday price. According to the Vinegar Institute, vinegar will keep almost indefinitely if stored in a cool, dark place. So don't worry about picking up more than you'll use every day. This is one ingredient you can tuck away and enjoy experimenting with in new recipes for marinades, dressings, and sauces — without breaking the bank!

INGREDIENTS

12	pork loin chops, boneless or bone-in (6–8 pounds)
½	cup prepared mustard
¼	cup lemon juice
¼	cup red wine vinegar
¼	cup vegetable oil
2	tablespoons honey
3	teaspoons minced garlic
3	teaspoons dried oregano

PACK IT UP
Three 1-gallon freezer bags, labeled

TURKISH PORK LOIN CHOPS
WITH BACON

MAKES 2 freezer meals, 5–6 servings each

INGREDIENTS

- 12   pork loin chops, boneless or bone-in (6–8 pounds)
- ¼   cup Turkish seasoning (try our homemade version below)
- 12–15   slices bacon

PACK IT UP

15–20 toothpicks

Two 1-gallon freezer bags, labeled

When I moved back to the Portland metropolitan area, one of my first adventures was to the Penzeys spice store on the other side of town. I couldn't resist the Turkish spice blend. If the Penzeys Turkish blend isn't easily available, you can try our homemade version below — it doesn't contain sumac like theirs does, but it still makes a mighty tasty chop. — KN

1 Trim chops as desired.

2 Rub 1 teaspoon Turkish seasoning over surfaces of each chop. Wrap one or more slices of bacon around edge of each chop, securing with toothpicks.

3 Place wrapped chops on a rimmed baking sheet and place in the freezer for 1 hour. Divide frozen chops evenly among freezer bags. To avoid puncturing bags, you might wish to double-bag the chops.

4 Seal and return to freezer. Food will stay at optimal quality for up to 3 months in freezer.

TO COOK ONE FREEZER MEAL

1 Place chops in an ungreased baking dish. Cover and completely thaw in refrigerator.

2 Preheat oven to 350°F (180°C).

3 Bake chops, uncovered, for 45 to 60 minutes, or until an instant-read thermometer inserted into thickest part of a chop reads 145°F (63°C).

HOMEMADE TURKISH SEASONING

Make your own seasoning by mixing together the following spices: 1 tablespoon ground cumin, 1 tablespoon garlic granules, 1 tablespoon salt, 2 teaspoons black pepper, 2 teaspoons dried oregano, 1 teaspoon dried cilantro, ½ teaspoon cayenne pepper.

BAKING DISH SIZES

Two to four chops will fit nicely in a 9-inch square baking dish.
If cooking five or more chops, use a 13- by 9-inch baking dish.

CAM'S RIBS

MAKES 3 freezer meals, 6 servings each

One of the best gifts I've ever received is a homemade cookbook from my friend Tamara. Filled with her favorite recipes and penned in her own funky handwriting, it has served to inspire many meals. Tamara is the kind of friend a person wants to emulate — not just in cooking but in all of life — with her fortitude, thoughtfulness, humor, and love. This recipe, named for her friend Cam, has been changed a bit to reflect my own tastes, but it retains its original name. — LA

1 Place the ribs in a large stockpot and cover with water. Simmer ribs until tender, about 1 hour. Drain, then divide ribs evenly among freezer bags.

2 In a large bowl, whisk together ketchup, sugar, vinegar, Worcestershire, mustard, garlic, onion, and pepper. Divide sauce evenly among bags of ribs.

3 Seal and freeze. Food will stay at optimal quality for up to 3 months in freezer.

TO COOK ONE FREEZER MEAL

1 Completely thaw one freezer meal in refrigerator.

2 Preheat oven to 350°F (180°C).

3 Pour ribs and sauce into an ungreased baking dish. Bake, uncovered, for 1 hour, basting ribs with sauce every 10 minutes.

INGREDIENTS

- 9 pounds boneless country-style ribs
- 3 cups ketchup
- 1½ cups firmly packed brown sugar
- 1½ cups red wine vinegar
- 1½ cups Worcestershire sauce
- 1½ tablespoons dry mustard
- 1½ tablespoons minced garlic
- 1½ tablespoons minced onion
- 1½ teaspoons black pepper

PACK IT UP
Three 1-gallon freezer bags, labeled

STICKY RIBS

MAKES 3 freezer meals, 6 servings each

The original version of this dish, and a lot of my cooking knowledge, came from my mom. The aroma that fills the house when these ribs are baking is terrific. — LA

---

1 Place the ribs in a large stockpot and cover with water. Simmer ribs until tender, about 1 hour. Drain and divide ribs evenly among freezer bags.

2 Into each bag, measure ¾ cup brown sugar, 1 cup water, ¼ cup soy sauce, and 1 tablespoon garlic.

3 Seal and gently shake each bag to combine contents. Freeze. Food will stay at optimal quality for up to 3 months in freezer.

TO COOK ONE FREEZER MEAL

1 Completely thaw one freezer meal in refrigerator.

2 Preheat oven to 350°F (180°C).

3 Pour ribs and sauce into an ungreased baking dish. Bake, uncovered, for about 1 hour, or until sauce is thick and sticky.

INGREDIENTS

- 9 pounds boneless country-style ribs
- 2¼ cups firmly packed brown sugar
- 3 cups water
- ¾ cup soy sauce
- 3 tablespoons minced garlic

PACK IT UP

Three 1-gallon freezer bags, labeled

FIREHOUSE PORK SKEWERS

MAKES 3 freezer meals, 6 servings each

INGREDIENTS

4½ pounds pork tenderloin

2 cups cider vinegar

1½ tablespoons jalapeño hot sauce

1 tablespoon soy sauce

1 tablespoon Worcestershire sauce

1½ teaspoons black pepper

1½ teaspoons red pepper flakes

1½ cups chopped onion (about 1 large)

ON HAND FOR COOKING EACH FREEZER MEAL

1 medium onion, cut into 8 wedges

10–12 (9-inch) wooden or metal skewers

PACK IT UP
Three 1-gallon freezer bags, labeled

Here's a tangy dish that's just a bit spicy. If you prefer your food with less kick, reduce the amount of red pepper flakes or jalapeño sauce. If you want the meat less tangy, replace ⅔ to 1 cup of the cider vinegar with an equal amount of chicken broth. — KN

1 Trim tenderloin as desired. Cut into 1-inch cubes. Divide evenly among freezer bags.

2 In a medium bowl, whisk together vinegar, hot sauce, soy sauce, and Worcestershire. Divide marinade evenly over pork. Into each bag, measure ½ teaspoon black pepper, ½ teaspoon red pepper flakes, and ½ cup onion.

3 Seal and gently shake each bag to combine contents. Freeze. Food will stay at optimal quality for up to 3 months in freezer.

TO COOK ONE FREEZER MEAL

1 Completely thaw one freezer meal in refrigerator.

2 Prepare a medium fire in a gas or charcoal grill.

3 If using wooden skewers, soak them in water while meat is thawing. Thread pork pieces and onion onto skewers. Grill for 12 to 15 minutes, turning occasionally, until thoroughly cooked. Discard remaining marinade.

CARIBBEAN
PORK TENDERLOIN

MAKES 3 freezer meals, 6 servings each

This is such a tasty dish, you'll be tempted to have it on hand throughout the year. — KN

1 Trim tenderloin as desired. Place 1½ pounds pork (or one-third of meat) into each freezer bag.

2 In a large bowl, whisk together vinegar, sugar, and soy sauce. Divide marinade evenly over pork. Into each bag, measure 1 teaspoon allspice, 1 teaspoon salt, 1 teaspoon thyme, ¼ teaspoon pepper, and ¼ teaspoon cinnamon. Gently shake each bag to distribute spices. Into each bag, measure 1 cup scallions, ½ cup onion, 1 tablespoon ginger, and 1 teaspoon garlic.

3 Seal and gently shake each bag to combine contents. Freeze. Food will stay at optimal quality for up to 3 months in freezer.

TO COOK ONE FREEZER MEAL

1 Completely thaw one freezer meal in refrigerator.

2 Prepare a medium-low fire in a gas or charcoal grill.

3 Lightly coat grill rack with cooking spray. Grill tenderloin for 15 to 18 minutes, or until an instant-read thermometer inserted into thickest part of pork reads 145°F (63°C). Discard remaining marinade.

INGREDIENTS

4½	pounds pork tenderloin
⅓	cup white vinegar
3	tablespoons firmly packed brown sugar
3	tablespoons soy sauce
3	teaspoons ground allspice
3	teaspoons salt
3	teaspoons dried thyme
¾	teaspoon black pepper
¾	teaspoon ground cinnamon
18	scallions, chopped (about 3 cups)
1½	cups chopped onion (about 1 large)
3	tablespoons minced ginger
3	teaspoons minced garlic

ON HAND FOR COOKING EACH FREEZER MEAL

Vegetable cooking spray

> **PACK IT UP**
> *Three 1-gallon freezer bags, labeled*

APPLE AND CRANBERRY
PORK SIRLOIN ROAST

MAKES 4 freezer meals, 6 servings each

INGREDIENTS

- 8 pounds pork sirloin tip roasts (4 roasts)
- 6 medium tart apples, peeled, cored, and sliced (about 8 cups)
- ⅔ cup apple jelly
- 4 cups diced onion (about 2 large)
- 1 cup dried cranberries
- 4 tablespoons cider vinegar
- 4 teaspoons dry mustard

This is the ultimate autumn dish! When everyone arrives home from a busy day and the sun has already gone down, the comforting aroma of simmered apples drifts from the oven and lifts your spirits. This dish has simple, mild flavors.

1 Trim sirloin roasts as desired. Place 1 roast into each freezer bag.

2 Divide apple slices and apple jelly evenly over roasts. Into each bag, measure 1 cup onion, ¼ cup cranberries, 1 tablespoon vinegar, and 1 teaspoon mustard.

3 Seal and freeze. Food will stay at optimal quality for up to 3 months in freezer.

TO COOK ONE FREEZER MEAL

1 Completely thaw one freezer meal in refrigerator.

2 Preheat oven to 350°F (180°C).

3 Place roast in center of an ungreased baking dish, distributing apples and onions around meat. Bake, uncovered, for 1 hour, or until an instant-read thermometer inserted into thickest part of roast reads 145°F (63°C).

PACK IT UP

Four 1-gallon freezer bags, labeled

APPLE JELLY

The apple jelly for this recipe is commonly found in 10-ounce and 18-ounce jars. If you buy the 10-ounce jar, you can use it all without measuring.

PORK LOIN
WITH APRICOT-SAUSAGE STUFFING

MAKES 3 freezer meals, 6–8 servings each

This recipe is the happy result of several brains working together. I found the sausages and came up with the initial concept, my friends Shawnee and Mike worked on it, and a star was born. The sauce makes this dish special. — KN

1 Trim loin as desired. Cut loin into three equal roasts. With one hand held flat across top of each roast, use a sharp knife to cut a pocket in middle of pork. Take care to cut up to, but not through, end of roast and to leave sides intact. (Pockets will be stuffed later.) Place 1 roast into each 1-gallon freezer bag.

2 In a medium bowl, combine apricots, sausages, and onion; divide evenly among three 1-quart freezer bags. Seal.

3 In a medium bowl, whisk together mustard and honey; divide evenly among three remaining 1-quart bags. Seal.

4 Place a bag of stuffing and a bag of sauce directly into each bag with roast. Seal and freeze. Food will stay at optimal quality for up to 3 months in freezer.

TO COOK ONE FREEZER MEAL

1 Completely thaw one freezer meal in refrigerator. Stuff roast pocket with apricot mixture.

2 Preheat oven to 350°F (180°C).

3 Place roast in an ungreased baking dish. Spread sauce over roast, covering completely. Bake, uncovered, for 45 to 60 minutes, or until an instant-read thermometer inserted into stuffing and thickest part of roast reads 145°F (63°C).

4 When roast is done, transfer drippings to a small saucepan and simmer until liquid reduces by about half. Stir in sour cream and spoon over pork slices.

INGREDIENTS

- 8 pounds pork loin (do not use tied pork loin roast)
- 1½ cups dried apricots, chopped
- 6 links chicken-apple sausage (such as Aidells), diced
- ¾ cup diced onion (about 1 small)
- ¾ cup Dijon mustard
- ¾ cup honey

ON HAND FOR COOKING EACH FREEZER MEAL

- ¼ cup sour cream

PACK IT UP

Three 1-gallon freezer bags, labeled

Six 1-quart freezer bags

PORK STEW

MAKES 3 freezer meals, 6 servings each

INGREDIENTS

1   pork loin (about 8 pounds; do not use tied pork loin roast)

¼   cup vegetable oil

5   pounds onions, chopped

1   cup water

¼   cup beef base

¼   cup minced garlic

3   tablespoons dried thyme

2   tablespoons paprika

2   teaspoons salt

2   teaspoons black pepper

I'm a firm believer that simple is most often best. This pork stew transforms common ingredients into a hearty and satisfying meal. Serve over hot rice. — LA

1 Trim loin as desired. Cut pork into small cubes, removing all visible fat. Divide evenly among freezer bags.

2 In a large stockpot, heat oil over medium heat. Add onions and cook, stirring occasionally, until soft, about 15 minutes. Add water and stir. Add beef base, garlic, thyme, paprika, salt, and pepper. Cook, stirring occasionally, for 10 minutes longer. Cool.

3 Divide cooled onion mixture evenly over pork.

4 Seal and freeze. Food will stay at optimal quality for up to 4 months in freezer.

TO COOK ONE FREEZER MEAL

1 Completely thaw one freezer meal in refrigerator.

2 In a large stockpot, combine pork mixture with 1½ cups water. Cook stew over medium heat until pork is completely cooked through and sauce has thickened, 30 to 40 minutes. Add more water during cooking if stew becomes dry.

> **PACK IT UP**
> *Three 1-gallon freezer bags, labeled*

PORK LOIN RAGOUT

MAKES 3 freezer meals, 6–8 servings each

Simmered in the slow cooker all day, this roast separates easily with a fork. Serve it over pasta or cheese ravioli. Or cook and shred one roast to make two pans of the Pork Ragout Lasagna on page 132. — KN

INGREDIENTS

- 2 tablespoons granulated garlic
- 1 tablespoon dried basil
- 1 tablespoon dried oregano
- ½ teaspoon salt
- ½ teaspoon black pepper
- 8 pounds pork loin (do not use tied pork loin roast)
- 9 cups (72 ounces) marinara sauce (try our Basic Red Sauce on page 190)
- 6 tablespoons balsamic or red wine vinegar
- 6 bay leaves
- 2 large onions, coarsely chopped
- 2 large green bell peppers, coarsely chopped

1 In a small bowl, mix together garlic, basil, oregano, salt, and black pepper. Set aside.

2 Trim loin as desired. Cut loin into three equal roasts. Rub each roast with one-third of garlic seasoning mixture. Place one roast into each unlabeled 1-gallon freezer bag.

3 Over each roast, measure 3 cups marinara sauce, 2 tablespoons vinegar, and 2 bay leaves. Seal bag.

4 Divide onions and bell peppers evenly among 1-quart freezer bags. Seal. Place a bag of pork and sauce and a bag of peppers and onions into each labeled 1-gallon bag.

5 Seal and freeze. Food will stay at optimal quality for up to 3 months in freezer.

TO COOK ONE FREEZER MEAL

1 Completely thaw one freezer meal in refrigerator.

2 Put onions and peppers into a slow cooker. Place roast and sauce on top. Cook on low for 8 to 10 hours.

3 Remove and discard bay leaves. Shred cooked pork with a fork, mix with sauce, and serve over pasta.

SEASONAL VARIATION: This dish happily accepts summer vegetables! Simply remove onions and bell peppers 30 minutes before mealtime. Then add ½ cup frozen peas and 1 small yellow squash, chopped. At mealtime, continue with cooking instructions in step 3 by removing bay leaves and cutting pork. Experiment with larger pieces of pork, rather than shredded.

PACK IT UP

Six 1-gallon freezer bags; label 3

Three 1-quart freezer bags

HONEY AND SPICE PORK KABOBS

MAKES 3 freezer meals, 6–8 servings each

If you are new to make-ahead meals, this is a great recipe for beginners. It can be halved for smaller families or those on a budget. I like to buy pork loin on sale to extend my savings. — KN

1 Trim loin as desired. Cut pork into 1-inch cubes; divide evenly among freezer bags.

2 In a medium bowl, whisk together orange juice, honey, cake spice, and salt. Divide marinade evenly over pork. Into each bag, measure 1 teaspoon minced garlic.

3 Seal and gently shake each bag to combine contents. Freeze. Food will stay at optimal quality for up to 3 months in freezer.

TO COOK ONE FREEZER MEAL

1 Completely thaw one freezer meal in refrigerator. If using wooden skewers, soak them in water while meat is thawing.

2 Prepare a medium-low fire in a gas or charcoal grill.

3 Thread pork pieces onto skewers. Grill, turning occasionally and basting as desired, for 15 to 18 minutes, or until thoroughly cooked. Do not baste during final 5 minutes of cooking. Discard remaining marinade.

HOMEMADE CAKE SPICE

Make your own seasoning by mixing together the following spices: 1 teaspoon ground cinnamon, ½ teaspoon ground allspice, ½ teaspoon ground anise, ½ teaspoon ground cloves, ½ teaspoon ground ginger, ½ teaspoon ground nutmeg.

Use the whole amount in the Honey and Spice Pork Kabobs, or as you like in your favorite baking.

INGREDIENTS

- 8 pounds pork loin (do not use tied pork loin roast)
- 3 cups orange juice
- 1½ cups honey
- 1 tablespoon cake spice (such as Penzeys, or try our homemade version below)
- 1½ teaspoons salt
- 3 teaspoons minced garlic

ON HAND FOR COOKING EACH FREEZER MEAL

- 10–12 (9-inch) wooden or metal skewers

PACK IT UP
Three 1-gallon freezer bags, labeled

PORK RAGOUT LASAGNA

MAKES 2 freezer meals, 12 servings each

INGREDIENTS

- 1 bag Pork Loin Ragout (page 130)
- 8 cups Basic Red Sauce (page 190)
- 1 (48-ounce) container cottage cheese (6 cups)
- 4 eggs, lightly beaten
- 2½ cups shredded Asiago cheese (8 ounces)
- 18–24 regular lasagna noodles, uncooked
- 6½ cups shredded mozzarella cheese (about 26 ounces)

PACK IT UP

Two 13- by 9- by 2-inch baking dishes

Plastic wrap

Aluminum foil

This recipe is my variation of Lindsay's Classic Lasagna recipe (page 79). She sent her original recipes with a brief note: "Work your magic with the ragout . . ." You'll notice I call for more noodles than Lindsay does in the original recipe. My pans are large, so it takes more to cover the bottom. Use the number of noodles required to cover the bottom of your pan in a single layer with no overlap. — KN

1 Cook Pork Loin Ragout according to directions on page 130. Remove roast from slow cooker and shred with a fork. Remove and discard bay leaves. Pour cooking juices into a large bowl. Add shredded pork and red sauce; mix well and set aside.

2 In a separate large bowl, mix cottage cheese, eggs, and 2 cups Asiago.

3 Lay baking dishes before you and assemble both lasagnas at once in layers in the following order:

Layer 1
- 4 uncooked noodles
- 2 cups pork sauce
- 2 cups cottage cheese mixture
- 1 cup mozzarella

Layer 2
- 4 uncooked noodles
- 2 cups pork sauce
- 2 cups cottage cheese mixture — or whatever remains
- 1 cup mozzarella

Layer 3
- 4 uncooked noodles
- 2 cups pork sauce — or whatever remains
- 1¼ cups mozzarella
- ¼ cup Asiago

4 Wrap each dish entirely in plastic wrap. Top with foil, label, and freeze. Food will stay at optimal quality for up to 3 months in freezer.

TO COOK ONE FREEZER MEAL

1 Completely thaw one freezer meal in refrigerator.

2 Preheat oven to 375°F (190°C).

3 Remove foil and plastic wrap from baking dish and replace foil. Bake for 50 minutes. Remove foil and continue baking for 20 to 30 minutes longer, or until center is hot and cheeses are browned. Remove from oven and let stand for 10 minutes before serving.

NOTE: This lasagna can be cooked without freezing; however, allow it to sit in refrigerator for a day or more so that noodles absorb liquid and soften before baking.

STICKY DRUNK
PIG ON A STICK

MAKES 3 freezer meals, 6–8 servings each

INGREDIENTS

8-9	pounds pork loin (do not use tied pork loin roast)
1½	cups bourbon
1½	cups honey
1½	cups lemon juice
1½	cups soy sauce
3	tablespoons olive oil
1½	cups chopped onion (about 1 large)
3	tablespoons minced ginger
3	teaspoons minced garlic
¾	teaspoon black pepper

ON HAND FOR COOKING EACH FREEZER MEAL

10-12 (9-inch) wooden or metal skewers

PACK IT UP

Three 1-gallon freezer bags, labeled

Honey and bourbon are the main attractions in this sassy dinner production. Clearly not a coat-and-tie dish, it's great for a casual cookout with family and friends. This recipe makes ample marinade for a pork loin weighing up to 9 pounds. — KN

---

1 Trim loin as desired. Cut pork into 1-inch cubes; divide evenly among freezer bags.

2 In a medium bowl, whisk together bourbon, honey, lemon juice, soy sauce, and oil. Divide marinade evenly over pork. Into each bag, measure ½ cup onion, 1 tablespoon ginger, 1 teaspoon garlic, and ¼ teaspoon pepper.

3 Seal and gently shake each bag to combine contents. Freeze. Food will stay at optimal quality for up to 3 months in freezer.

TO COOK ONE FREEZER MEAL

1 Completely thaw one freezer meal in refrigerator. If using wooden skewers, soak them in water while meat is thawing.

2 Prepare a medium-low fire in a gas or charcoal grill.

3 Thread pork pieces onto skewers. Grill for 15 to 18 minutes, turning occasionally and basting as desired, until thoroughly cooked. Do not baste during final 5 minutes of cooking. Discard remaining marinade.

COMMUNITY COOKING

One of the benefits of participating in a cooking club is sharing costs. Take the bourbon in this recipe. If you had to buy it yourself, you might skip making this dish entirely. But you may be tempted to try it if you're splitting the bill. For more discussion of cooking communities and their benefits, see page 235.

RAGING GARLIC
PORK STIR-FRY

MAKES 4 freezer meals, 4–6 servings each

This recipe is just as delicious with chicken breast or a tender cut of beef. The red pepper flakes add some heat — add more or less to suit your family's taste. Serve with stir-fried bok choy or broccoli. — LA

1 Trim sirloin roasts as desired. Cut pork into bite-size cubes; divide evenly among four 1-quart freezer bags. Seal.

2 In a medium bowl, whisk together soy sauce, vinegar, and sugar. Divide marinade evenly among four remaining 1-quart bags. Into each bag of sauce, measure 2 teaspoons garlic and ¼ teaspoon red pepper flakes. Seal and gently shake each bag to combine contents.

3 Into each 1-gallon freezer bag, place a bag of pork and a bag of sauce. Seal and freeze. Food will stay at optimal quality for up to 3 months in freezer.

TO COOK ONE FREEZER MEAL

1 Completely thaw one freezer meal in refrigerator.

2 Pour off and discard any accumulated liquid from bag of pork. Add cornstarch; seal bag and shake to coat meat.

3 In a large skillet, heat oil over medium-high heat. Add pork and stir-fry until thoroughly cooked, about 10 minutes.

INGREDIENTS

8	pounds pork sirloin tip roasts (4 roasts)
1½	cups soy sauce
½	cup white wine vinegar
2	tablespoons sugar
8	teaspoons minced garlic
1	teaspoon red pepper flakes, or to taste

ON HAND FOR COOKING EACH FREEZER MEAL

½	cup cornstarch
2	teaspoons vegetable oil

PACK IT UP

Eight 1-quart freezer bags

Four 1-gallon freezer bags, labeled

GARLIC-STUDDED PORK LOIN

MAKES 3 freezer meals, 6–8 servings each

INGREDIENTS

- 2 tablespoons dried oregano
- 1 tablespoon salt
- 1 tablespoon black pepper
- 8 pounds pork loin or pork sirloin tip roasts
- 18 garlic cloves
- ¾ cup lemon juice
- ¾ cup olive oil
- ¾ cup water

Come home and enjoy this Mediterranean-style roast after a busy day. Slow cooking your main dish leaves you a little extra time for finishing touches: a roasted head of garlic to spread on a fresh baguette, fresh mozzarella over sliced tomatoes topped with fresh basil leaves, or perhaps a simple spinach salad with red onion, pitted Kalamata olives, and feta. — KN

1 In a small bowl, mix together oregano, salt, and pepper. Set aside.

2 Trim loin as desired. Cut loin into three equal roasts. Using tip of a sharp paring knife, cut 12 openings ¾ inch deep in each roast. Slice each garlic clove in half and place one garlic piece in each opening.

3 Rub each roast with one-third of oregano mixture. Place 1 roast into each freezer bag. Over each roast, measure ¼ cup lemon juice, ¼ cup oil, and ¼ cup water.

4 Seal and freeze. Food will stay at optimal quality for up to 3 months in freezer.

TO COOK ONE FREEZER MEAL

Completely thaw one freezer meal in refrigerator. Put roast and marinade in a slow cooker and cook on low for 8 to 10 hours.

PACK IT UP

Three 1-gallon freezer bags, labeled

LEMON JUICE FROM CONCENTRATE

If you choose bottled lemon juice, take care to check the expiration date. While two-packs of lemon juice are three to five times less expensive per fluid ounce at the wholesale club, the juice does not keep indefinitely. If you purchase more than you will use in cooking, consider using it to clean around the house. Lemon is a natural cleaning agent and deodorizer.

ROASTED
POBLANO-POTATO SOUP

MAKES 4–6 servings

PREP AHEAD

2 cups shredded Garlic-Studded Pork Loin (page 136)

INGREDIENTS

2 poblano peppers

1 tablespoon olive oil

½ cup diced onion

1 pound yellow potatoes, peeled and diced

4 cups chicken broth

1 cup heavy cream

It's worth the small bit of extra effort to roast poblano peppers for this soup, but you can expedite the process by using two 7-ounce cans of diced green chiles instead. — LA

---

1 Turn on broiler.

2 Place peppers on a sheet pan and broil until skin is charred, turning as necessary to char peppers entirely. Remove peppers from oven, place in a paper bag, seal, and let steam for about 10 minutes. When peppers are cool enough to handle, use a paring knife to peel and scrape off as much charred skin as you can. Slice off stem and remove seeds, then chop peppers.

3 In a medium pot, heat oil over medium heat. Add onion and peppers, and cook, stirring often, until onions are soft and translucent, about 5 minutes.

4 Add pork, potatoes, and broth. Simmer until potatoes are tender, about 15 minutes.

5 Stir in cream and heat through. Remove from heat and serve.

FARMERS' MARKET SOUP

MAKES 3 freezer meals, 8 servings each

This hearty sausage and lentil soup comes together easily and is no extra work at dinnertime. (See photo on page 5.) — LA

1 In a large skillet or pot, brown sausage over medium heat until pork is no longer pink, about 15 minutes. Drain and discard fat. Cool.

2 Divide sausage evenly among freezer bags.

3 Wipe out skillet or pot and heat oil over medium heat. Add kale, carrots, onion, leeks, and celery, and cook, stirring occasionally, for 5 minutes. Cool, then evenly divide vegetable mixture over sausage in bags.

4 Into each bag, measure 4 cups broth, 1½ cups lentils, 2 tablespoons mustard, 1 tablespoon vinegar, 1 teaspoon salt, and ½ teaspoon pepper.

5 Seal and freeze. Food will stay at optimal quality for up to 4 months in freezer.

TO COOK ONE FREEZER MEAL

Slow Cooker

1 Put frozen or thawed soup into slow cooker.

2 Add 2 cups water.

3 Cook on low for 6 to 8 hours or on high for 3 to 4 hours.

Stovetop

1 Put frozen or thawed soup into pot.

2 Add 2 cups water.

3 Simmer over medium heat until lentils and vegetables are tender, about 40 minutes. Add additional water during cooking if desired.

INGREDIENTS

- 3 pounds ground mild Italian sausage
- 3 tablespoons olive oil
- 6 cups roughly chopped kale (discard thick stems)
- 3 cups chopped carrots (about 6 medium)
- 3 cups chopped onion (about 3 small)
- 1½ cups sliced leeks, white parts only (about 2 large)
- ¾ cup chopped celery (about 2 stalks)
- 12 cups chicken broth
- 4½ cups dried lentils
- 6 tablespoons spicy brown mustard
- 3 tablespoons apple cider vinegar
- 3 teaspoons salt
- 1½ teaspoons black pepper

PACK IT UP

Three 1-gallon freezer bags, labeled

CHILE VERDE

MAKES 4 freezer meals, 5 servings each

INGREDIENTS

- 9 pounds pork sirloin tip roasts or pork loin
- 2 cups all-purpose flour
- ½ cup vegetable oil
- 6 cups chopped onions (about 6 medium)
- 2 (14.5-ounce) cans diced tomatoes or 3–4 large fresh tomatoes
- 2 (7-ounce) cans whole green chiles or 8–10 small fresh mild green chiles
- 4 tomatillos, husks removed
- 1 large green bell pepper, stem and seeds removed
- 4 cups loosely packed chopped cilantro
- 4 large cloves garlic
- 2 tablespoons ground cumin
- 1 tablespoon salt
- 2 cups water

This flavorful pork stew is one of my all-time favorites. If you have fresh, flavorful ripe red tomatoes, and fresh mild green chiles, use those in place of the canned products. — LA

1 Trim pork as desired. Cut pork into bite-size cubes and place in a large bowl. Toss pork pieces with enough flour to coat their surface.

2 In a large skillet, heat 2 tablespoons vegetable oil over medium heat. Working in batches so pan does not crowd, brown pork on all sides. Set browned pork aside to cool and add more oil to pan as necessary. Finish browning remaining batches of pork.

3 Add onions to same skillet and cook over medium heat, stirring often, until onions are soft and develop a deep golden color, about 12 minutes. Set onions aside to cool.

4 Meanwhile, in a blender or food processor, combine tomatoes, chiles, tomatillos, bell pepper, cilantro, garlic, cumin, and salt, and blend until a smooth sauce forms, about 15 seconds.

5 Divide pork, onions, and blended sauce evenly among freezer bags. To each bag, add ½ cup water.

6 Seal and freeze. Food will stay at optimal quality for up to 4 months in freezer.

TO COOK ONE FREEZER MEAL
Chile verde can be cooked when frozen or thawed.

Stovetop
In a medium saucepan, cook meat and sauce, stirring occasionally, over medium heat until pork is very tender and sauce is thickened, about 2 hours.

Slow Cooker
Cook on low until pork is very tender, 4 to 6 hours. Sauce will be thinner if cooked in a slow cooker.

PACK IT UP

Four 1-gallon freezer bags, labeled

SMOKED GOUDA AND HAM
STRATA

MAKES 3 freezer meals, 6 servings each

Savory stratas and galettes are very enjoyable brunch fare. I created this dish for Christmas brunch a number of years ago, but I make it any time of year now. It's especially nice to have a dish like this at the ready for those Saturday mornings when everyone decides to sleep in after a busy week. Leftovers reheat nicely in the microwave. — KN

1 Arrange greased baking dishes in a row.

2 Cut one loaf of bread into 1-inch cubes. Divide bread cubes evenly among greased dishes, making sure to cover bottoms.

3 Spread ¾ cup Gouda and ½ cup ham over bread in each dish.

4 Cut remaining loaf into 1-inch cubes. Divide cubes evenly among pans. Finish layering with ¾ cup cheese and ½ cup ham in each pan.

5 In a medium bowl, whisk together 6 eggs, ⅔ cup milk, and ½ teaspoon onion powder. Pour over bread mixture in one pan. Repeat for remaining pans.

6 Cover each baking dish generously with plastic wrap, then foil. Label and freeze. Place bags of frozen vegetables or other items on top of foil while freezing to press bread cubes into egg mixture. Food will stay at optimal quality for up to 3 months in freezer.

TO COOK ONE FREEZER MEAL

1 Completely thaw one freezer meal in refrigerator.

2 Preheat oven to 350°F (180°C).

3 Remove foil and plastic wrap from baking dish and replace foil.

4 Bake for 25 minutes. Remove foil and bake for 5 to 10 minutes longer, until top begins to brown.

INGREDIENTS

- 2 loaves Italian bread (1–1½ pounds each)
- 12 ounces smoked Gouda cheese, shredded (about 4½ cups)
- 14 ounces deli sliced ham, chopped
- 18 eggs
- 2 cups milk
- 1½ teaspoons onion powder

PACK IT UP

Three 8- by 2-inch square baking dishes, greased

Plastic wrap

Aluminum foil

VEGGIE AND SEAFOOD

MAINS, SIDES, AND SOUPS

ASPARAGUS AND POTATO
FRITTATA

MAKES 3 freezer meals, 6–8 servings each

INGREDIENTS

2 pounds fresh asparagus, cleaned and fibrous ends snapped off

3 pounds yellow-flesh potatoes, boiled and cut into bite-size pieces

1 cup chopped onion (about 1 medium)

18 eggs

1½ cups heavy cream

1½ teaspoons salt

¾ teaspoon black pepper

This hot dish makes a delicious light dinner. It's equally ideal for breakfast or brunch. — LA

---

1 Place asparagus in a large shallow pan with just enough water to cover. Bring to a boil. Reduce heat and simmer for 2 minutes. Plunge asparagus into cold water to cool quickly. Cut asparagus into bite-size pieces. Divide asparagus, potatoes, and onion among freezer bags.

2 In a medium bowl, lightly beat 6 eggs. Add ½ cup cream, ½ teaspoon salt, and ¼ teaspoon pepper. Pour into one freezer bag and seal. Repeat for two remaining frittatas.

3 Freeze. Food will stay at optimal quality for up to 2 months in freezer.

TO COOK ONE FREEZER MEAL

1 Completely thaw one freezer meal in refrigerator.

2 Preheat oven to 425°F (220°C).

3 Pour frittata into a lightly greased 8-inch square baking dish. Bake for 30 minutes, or until egg is cooked through and top is golden brown.

PACK IT UP

Three 1-gallon freezer bags, labeled

RICE PILAF

MAKES 4 freezer sides, 4–6 servings each

This quick and tasty side dish is a welcome change from plain rice. Pair it with any of our grilled beef, chicken, or pork entrées. — LA

1 In a large skillet, heat oil and butter over medium heat. Add rice, carrots, celery, and onion; cook, stirring, until rice is golden brown, 5 to 7 minutes. Cool.

2 Divide rice mixture among freezer bags. Into each bag, measure 2 teaspoons chicken base, 1 teaspoon parsley, and ¼ teaspoon pepper.

3 Seal and freeze. Food will stay at optimal quality for up to 3 months in freezer.

TO COOK ONE SIDE DISH

Place frozen pilaf in a medium saucepan and add 3 cups water. Bring to a boil; reduce heat and cook, covered, until water is completely absorbed, about 20 minutes.

INGREDIENTS

- ¼ cup olive oil
- 2 tablespoons butter
- 6 cups white rice, uncooked
- 2 cups chopped carrots (about 4 medium)
- 1 cup chopped celery (about 4 stalks)
- 1 cup chopped onion (about 1 medium)
- 8 teaspoons chicken base
- 4 teaspoons dried parsley
- 1 teaspoon black pepper

PACK IT UP

Four 1-gallon freezer bags, labeled

MORE VEGGIE OPTIONS

We've included more veggie recipes in the Sauces, Marinades, and Flavored Butters chapter:

- Portobello Mushrooms with Asian Market Marinade (page 181)

- Fresh Vegetable Stir-Fry with Asian Marinated Tofu (page 182)

- Lemony Caesar Portobello Mushrooms (page 184)

- Maple Portobello Mushrooms (page 187)

- Green Beans with Gorgonzola-Pecan Butter (page 196)

- Butternut Squash with Gorgonzola-Pecan Butter (page 198)

- Linguine with Roasted Sweet Potato and Gorgonzola Lemon-Pepper Butter (page 202)

SKILLET RICE AND BEANS

MAKES 8 freezer meals, 6–8 servings each

INGREDIENTS

- ⅔ cup vegetable oil
- ⅔ cup dried green bell pepper flakes (about 1½ ounces)
- 3 tablespoons crushed jalapeño pepper flakes, or more to taste
- ⅔ cup bold taco seasoning (try my homemade version, below)
- 2½ cups diced onion (about 2 medium)
- 10 cups white basmati rice, rinsed and well drained

ON HAND FOR COOKING EACH FREEZER MEAL

- 1 (14.5-ounce) can diced tomatoes
- 2 cups water
- 1 (15-ounce) can black beans, rinsed and drained

  Cheddar cheese (optional)

PACK IT UP

Eight 1-quart freezer bags, labeled

I began developing this brunch recipe nearly a decade ago. Leftovers reheat beautifully in the microwave at work, and it has been a hit at many potluck gatherings. It's so easy and economical to make that I can splurge a little with toppings, like specialty olives and locally produced salsas. Be aware that the recipe makes many freezer meals. It's best to use your largest stockpot. — KN

---

1 In a large stockpot, heat oil over medium heat. Add bell pepper flakes, crushed jalapeño flakes, and taco seasoning, and cook for 3 minutes.

2 Add onion and rice to stockpot and cook, stirring constantly, until rice is toasted, about 10 to 12 minutes.

3 Remove from heat and cool. Divide rice mixture among freezer bags.

4 Seal and freeze. Food will stay at optimal quality for up to 6 months in freezer.

TO COOK ONE FREEZER MEAL

1 Completely thaw one freezer meal in refrigerator.

2 In a 10-inch skillet, combine rice mixture, diced tomatoes, and 2 cups water. Cover and cook over medium-low heat until water is absorbed and rice is fluffy, about 25 minutes.

3 Mix in black beans. Remove from heat and serve immediately. Top with cheddar cheese, if desired.

HOMEMADE BOLD TACO SEASONING

Make your own taco seasoning by mixing together 3 tablespoons medium-hot chili powder, 2 tablespoons ground cumin, 2 tablespoons granulated garlic, 2 tablespoons Mexican oregano, 1 tablespoon onion salt, 1 tablespoon smoked Spanish paprika (or more to taste).

FETA AND SPINACH
LASAGNA ROLLS

MAKES 8 freezer meals, 6–8 rolls each

If you're looking for an interesting variation on the usual pan lasagna, these rolls will be a treat! Each noodle takes a heaping ⅛ cup of filling (about 3 tablespoons) and is then rolled instead of being layered in a pan. This dish is great for small and large families alike because you can pull out just the right number of rolls to cook for lunch on those busy weekend days. — KN

1 Working in batches, boil noodles until flexible enough to roll but not completely cooked.

2 Meanwhile, in a large bowl, mix feta, cottage cheese, ricotta, Asiago, Parmesan, and pepper. Stir in spinach.

3 Working in batches, place partially cooked noodles on a clean work surface in a single layer (do not overlap).

4 Spread 3 tablespoons filling down length of each noodle. Roll noodles and place seam side down on a rimmed baking sheet. Place rolls in freezer for 30 minutes.

5 Divide frozen rolls evenly among freezer bags. Seal and refreeze. Food will stay at optimal quality for up to 3 months in freezer.

TO COOK ONE FREEZER MEAL

1 Place eight lasagna rolls in greased baking dish. Cover with foil; completely thaw in refrigerator.

2 Preheat oven to 350°F (180°C).

3 Pour marinara over rolls and top with mozzarella; replace foil. Bake for 35 to 40 minutes, or until center is hot and cheese is melted.

RULE OF THUMB

Use a 9-inch square baking dish for up to eight rolls and a 13- by 9-inch baking dish for more than eight rolls. If cooking more than eight rolls, you'll need to increase the amounts for the sauce and mozzarella: For every four lasagna rolls, use 1 cup marinara sauce and ½ cup mozzarella.

INGREDIENTS

- 3½ (16-ounce) boxes regular lasagna noodles (15–18 noodles in each box)
- 1 (24-ounce) container crumbled feta cheese (about 5 cups)
- 1 (32-ounce) container low-fat cottage cheese (4 cups)
- 1 (32-ounce) container part-skim ricotta cheese (3½ cups)
- 1 cup shredded Asiago cheese (about 3 ounces)
- 1 cup shredded Parmesan cheese (about 3 ounces)
- 2 teaspoons black pepper
- 15 ounces frozen chopped spinach, broken apart and leaves separated

ON HAND FOR COOKING EACH FREEZER MEAL

- 1 *9-inch square baking dish, greased*

  Aluminum foil
- 2 cups marinara sauce (try our Basic Red Sauce on page 190)
- 1 cup shredded mozzarella cheese (about 4 ounces)

PACK IT UP
Eight 1-gallon freezer bags, labeled

LEMON-BLUEBERRY STRATA

MAKES 2 freezer meals, 8 servings each

INGREDIENTS

- 2 loaves Italian bread (1–1½ pounds each)
- 2 (8-ounce) packages cream cheese, softened
- 3 cups plus 3 tablespoons milk
- 1 tablespoon superfine sugar
- 1 tablespoon lemon extract
- 2 teaspoons minced, dried lemon peel
- 2½ cups frozen blueberries (about one 12-ounce bag)
- 18 eggs
- ⅔ cup maple syrup
- 1 teaspoon salt

PACK IT UP

Two 13- by 9- by 2-inch baking dishes, greased

Plastic wrap

Aluminum foil

My testers shared this brunch recipe with extended family on a weekend getaway. They reported that the kids asked for seconds and even thirds, and they were happy about leftovers for a change. Check the bulk spice and tea section of the grocery store for dried lemon peel. It's much more economical to buy just the amount you need. — KN

1 Cut bread into 1-inch cubes. Spread one-half of cubes evenly between greased baking dishes. Set remaining bread cubes aside.

2 In the bowl of a food processor, combine cream cheese, 3 tablespoons milk, sugar, lemon extract, and lemon peel. Process until smooth, scraping down sides of bowl as needed.

3 Spread one-half cream cheese mixture over bread in each dish, dividing evenly. Top with 1 cup blueberries, divided evenly.

4 Repeat layers, dividing all remaining bread cubes, cream cheese, and blueberries between dishes.

5 In a large bowl, combine 9 eggs, 1½ cups milk, ⅓ cup maple syrup, and ½ teaspoon salt. Pour egg mixture over layers in one baking dish. Repeat for second baking dish.

6 Cover each baking dish generously with plastic wrap and then foil. Label and freeze. Place bags of frozen vegetables or other items on top of foil while freezing to press bread cubes into egg mixture; remove items when frozen. Food will stay at optimal quality for up to 3 months in freezer.

TO BAKE ONE FREEZER MEAL

1 Completely thaw one freezer meal in refrigerator.

2 Preheat oven to 350°F (180°C).

3 Remove foil and plastic wrap from baking dish and replace foil.

4 Bake for 50 to 60 minutes, or until a toothpick inserted into center comes out clean. Cool for 5 minutes before serving. Enjoy with additional syrup, if desired.

WILD RICE AND NUT BAKE

MAKES 4 freezer meals, 6 servings each

Many families share their holiday dinner table with vegetarians and meat eaters alike. This is a wonderful side dish for turkey or ham. It can also provide a satisfying vegetarian entrée when accompanied by a fresh salad, steamed vegetables, or rolls. And it's a great way to use up any leftover roasted vegetables — I've even used roasted beets! — KN

1 In a large bowl, mix rice, cheese, milk, eggs, onion, sunflower seeds, pear, celery, and salt. The mixture will be wet.

2 Divide evenly among freezer bags.

3 Seal and freeze. Food will stay at optimal quality for up to 6 months in freezer.

TO COOK ONE FREEZER MEAL

1 Completely thaw one freezer meal in refrigerator.

2 Preheat oven to 350°F (180°C).

3 Into a large bowl, empty rice mixture and add roasted vegetables.

4 Pour mixture into a greased 8-inch square baking dish. Bake, uncovered, for 40 to 45 minutes, or until set and a knife inserted into center comes out clean.

INGREDIENTS

- 7 cups cooked wild rice blend, cooled (about 2½ cups uncooked rice blend)
- 6 cups Colby-Jack cheese blend (about 24 ounces)
- 3 cups milk
- 12 large eggs, lightly beaten
- 4 cups diced red onion (about 3 medium)
- 1½ cups sunflower seeds, roasted and unsalted
- 1½ cups diced firm pear (about 2 medium)
- 1 cup diced celery (about 3-4 medium stalks)
- 2 teaspoons salt

ON HAND FOR COOKING EACH FREEZER MEAL

- ½ cup savory roasted vegetables, such as Brussels sprouts or cauliflower

---

PACK IT UP

Four 1-gallon freezer bags, labeled

PHYLLO DOUGH

Phyllo can seem fussy, but it's really quite forgiving. Though the sheets are paper-thin and can tear, the pastry is easily patched. Because this recipe calls for two sheets to be stacked and the final product is folded over and over, any damage to the dough is concealed.

SPANAKOPITA

MAKES 3 freezer meals, 4–5 servings each

I grew up in a city where eating out meant visiting any one of a number of small, family-owned ethnic restaurants. Always a culinary adventure! I never tired of the Mediterranean food served in my favorite Greek restaurant. Keep these savory pockets on hand for lunch, a light dinner, or even a snack. — LA

1 In a large stockpot, wilt spinach over medium heat. Do not overcook. Drain and cool.

2 Using your hands, squeeze as much water from spinach as possible. Place spinach in a large bowl; stir in eggs, lemon juice, dill, salt, and pepper.

3 Lay one sheet of phyllo dough on a clean work surface. Using a pastry brush, dab all over with melted butter; lay a second sheet on top. Cut dough in half lengthwise.

4 Lay the two strips, with narrow edges nearest you, on work surface. Place ¼ to ⅓ cup spinach mixture at bottom of each strip of dough. Top with 1 tablespoon feta.

5 Fold dough flag-style to form triangle-shaped packets: Fold bottom-right corner to left edge of dough to form a triangle. Fold triangle along left edge of dough, then fold lower-left corner to right edge of dough. Seal any remaining top edge of dough to packet. Filling should be totally enclosed in dough.

6 Wrap each pastry individually in plastic wrap. Divide evenly among freezer bags.

7 Seal and freeze. Food will stay at optimal quality for up to 2 months in freezer.

INGREDIENTS

- 2½ pounds fresh spinach, rinsed, with water still clinging to leaves
- 2 eggs, lightly beaten
- ¼ cup lemon juice
- ¼ cup chopped fresh dill or 4 teaspoons dried
- 1 teaspoon salt
- 1 teaspoon black pepper
- 14–16 sheets phyllo dough
- 2 tablespoons melted butter
- 1 cup crumbled feta cheese (about 5 ounces)

ON HAND FOR BAKING

- 2 teaspoons melted butter for each pastry

PACK IT UP

Plastic wrap

Three 1-gallon freezer bags, labeled

TO BAKE

1 Thaw pastries in refrigerator or bake straight from freezer.

2 Preheat oven to 400°F (200°C).

3 Remove as many pastries as desired from freezer. Remove plastic wrap. Place pastries on a greased baking sheet. Brush with melted butter. Bake for 17 to 19 minutes if frozen, 14 to 16 minutes if thawed.

ROASTED SWEET POTATO AND BLACK BEAN
ENCHILADA STACK

MAKES 3 freezer meals, 4 servings each

INGREDIENTS

- 2 pounds poblano peppers (about 6 large)
- 3 pounds sweet potatoes or yams (about 3 large), peeled and cut into ½-inch cubes
- ¼ cup plus 2 tablespoons olive oil
- 2 teaspoons salt
- 2 cups chopped onion (about 2 medium)
- 1 tablespoon minced garlic
- 4 cups vegetable broth
- 2 tablespoons cornstarch
- 2 tablespoons water
- 18 corn tortillas
- 2 (15-ounce) cans black beans, drained and rinsed
- 2 cups Monterey jack cheese (about 8 ounces)

PACK IT UP

Three 8-inch square foil pans

Plastic wrap

Aluminum foil

Roasted poblano peppers make a mildly spicy green sauce in this vegetarian recipe. Bonus — it's gluten free! If you are looking for a dairy-free or vegan recipe, leave out the cheese. If you love the flavors of sweet potato and black bean but would like something more saucy, layer these with the suiza sauce on page 66. — LA

---

1 Turn on broiler. To roast poblano peppers, place peppers on a sheet pan and broil for about 5 minutes, or until skin is charred, turning as necessary to char peppers entirely. Remove peppers from oven, place in a paper bag, seal, and let steam for about 10 minutes.

2 When peppers are cool enough to handle, use a paring knife to peel and scrape off as much charred skin as you can. Slice off stems, remove seeds, then chop peppers. Set aside.

3 Preheat oven to 425°F (220°C).

4 On a rimmed baking sheet, toss sweet potatoes with 2 tablespoons oil and 1 teaspoon salt. Bake for 20 to 25 minutes, or until soft and beginning to brown on edges.

5 In a large skillet, add onions and remaining ¼ cup oil, and cook, stirring, over medium heat until onions soften and begin to turn golden brown, about 15 minutes. Add roasted peppers and garlic, and cook, stirring, 5 minutes longer.

6 Add broth and simmer over medium-low heat, uncovered, for 25 minutes. In a small bowl, combine cornstarch and water, and mix until smooth. Whisk cornstarch slurry into sauce. Cook, stirring, until thickened and smooth, about 5 minutes.

7 Spread ¼ cup sauce over bottom of each pan. Cover bottom of each pan with 2 tortillas, tearing them to fit in one layer. Divide half of sweet potatoes and half of beans evenly among each pan. Sprinkle 2 tablespoons cheese in each pan. Top with ¼ cup sauce.

8 Repeat layers one more time in each pan, with 2 more tortillas, remaining sweet potatoes, remaining beans, 2 tablespoons cheese, and ¼ cup sauce. Finish with 2 tortillas in each pan and divide remaining sauce and cheese among pans.

9 Wrap each dish entirely in plastic wrap. Top with foil, label, and freeze. Food will stay at optimal quality for up to 3 months in freezer.

TO COOK ONE FREEZER MEAL

1 Completely thaw one dish in refrigerator.

2 Preheat oven to 350°F (180°C).

3 Remove foil and plastic wrap from baking dish and replace foil. Bake, covered, for 25 minutes. Remove foil and bake for 5 to 10 minutes longer, or until sauce is bubbling.

THAI RED CURRY
WITH VEGETABLES

MAKES 2 freezer meals, 4 servings each

INGREDIENTS

2   (13.5-ounce) cans coconut milk

½   cup chicken broth

2   tablespoons fish sauce

2   teaspoons red curry paste

1   teaspoon honey

½   pound fresh white mushrooms, cleaned and sliced

1   cup sliced carrots (about 2 medium)

1   (15-ounce) can baby corn, drained

1   (8-ounce) can bamboo shoots, drained

PACK IT UP
Two 1-gallon freezer bags, labeled

This dish is on the spicy side. The red curry paste supplies all the heat, so adjust that ingredient if you want less fire. This recipe can be served over rice as an entrée or to complement a meal as a side dish. If serving as a side dish, divide ingredients between three 1-gallon freezer bags, not two. — LA

---

1 In a medium saucepan, combine coconut milk, broth, fish sauce, curry paste, and honey over medium heat. Add mushrooms; cook, stirring, for 5 minutes. Add carrots; cook, stirring, for 5 minutes. Cool.

2 Divide cooled vegetable mixture evenly among freezer bags. Divide corn and bamboo shoots evenly over vegetables.

3 Seal and freeze. Food will stay at optimal quality for up to 3 months in freezer.

TO COOK ONE FREEZER MEAL

1 Completely thaw one bag in refrigerator.

2 In a medium saucepan, warm sauce and vegetables over medium heat.

SHRIMP CURRY

MAKES 3 freezer meals, 4–6 servings each

Large prawns or tiny bay shrimp work equally well in this seafood version of our popular Chicken Curry. Serve over rice with any of the following toppings: toasted shredded coconut, toasted sliced almonds, apple pieces, pineapple tidbits, raisins, dried cranberries, chopped scallions, mango chutney, hot chili paste, or sweet chili sauce. If using frozen cooked shrimp, be sure to freeze separately from the sauce so the delicate shrimp don't thaw. — LA

1 In a large saucepan, melt butter over medium heat. Add onion and cook, stirring, until soft, about 5 minutes. Add curry, chicken base, garlic, ginger, sugar, and salt; cook, stirring, for 2 minutes. Add flour; cook, stirring, for 2 minutes longer. Mixture will be like a paste.

2 Gradually add milk and water, and cook, stirring constantly, until sauce has thickened. Add lemon juice only after sauce has thickened. Cool sauce.

If Using Fresh Cooked Shrimp

1 Divide shrimp evenly among three labeled freezer bags. Divide cooled sauce evenly over shrimp.

2 Seal and freeze. Food will stay at optimal quality for up to 2 months in freezer.

If Using Frozen Cooked Shrimp

1 Divide shrimp evenly among three unlabeled freezer bags. Divide cooled sauce evenly among three other unlabeled bags. Seal bags. Into each labeled bag, place a bag of shrimp and a bag of sauce.

2 Seal and freeze. Food will stay at optimal quality for up to 2 months in freezer.

TO COOK ONE FREEZER MEAL

1 Completely thaw one freezer meal in refrigerator.

2 In a large skillet over medium heat, bring shrimp and curry sauce to a simmer. Do not boil.

INGREDIENTS

- 1 cup (2 sticks) butter
- 2 cups chopped onion (about 2 medium)
- ¼ cup curry powder
- 2 tablespoons chicken base
- 2 tablespoons minced garlic
- 2 tablespoons minced ginger
- 2 tablespoons sugar
- 1 tablespoon salt
- 1½ cups all-purpose flour
- 4 cups milk
- 4 cups water
- 2 tablespoons lemon juice
- 2 pounds cleaned and cooked prawns or shrimp, fresh or frozen

> **PACK IT UP**
> *Three to nine 1-gallon freezer bags; label 3*

MANICOTTI

MAKES 4 freezer meals, 4 servings each

INGREDIENTS

- 1 (48-ounce) container cottage cheese (6 cups)
- 2 eggs, lightly beaten
- 3 cups shredded mozzarella cheese (about 12 ounces)
- 1 cup shredded Parmesan cheese (about 4 ounces)
- ½ teaspoon salt
- ½ teaspoon black pepper
- 2 (8-ounce) boxes manicotti (12–14 shells in each box), uncooked
- 12 cups Basic Red Sauce (page 189)

Once I discovered how much easier it is to make lasagna by using uncooked noodles, I decided to revisit manicotti; I had long ago given up on struggling with the limp, easily torn cooked manicotti noodles. This recipe is easy to put together and is a favorite go-to for a meatless entrée. — LA

1 In a large bowl, mix cottage cheese, eggs, mozzarella, Parmesan, salt, and pepper. With your fingers, a spoon, or a piping bag with a large nozzle, stuff filling into manicotti shells.

2 Spread ½ cup red sauce in bottom of each baking dish. Place 6 or 7 manicotti in each dish. Divide remaining red sauce evenly over four dishes of manicotti. Wrap each dish entirely in plastic wrap.

3 Top with foil, label, and freeze. Food will stay at optimal quality for up to 2 months in freezer.

TO COOK ONE FREEZER MEAL

1 Thaw one freezer meal in refrigerator or bake it straight from freezer.

2 Preheat oven to 350°F (180°C).

3 Remove foil and plastic wrap from baking dish and replace foil. Bake for 45 minutes if thawed, 1 hour if frozen. Remove foil and continue baking until noodles are tender.

PACK IT UP

Four 8-inch square baking dishes

Plastic wrap

Aluminum

VEGETABLE LASAGNA
LARGE PAN

MAKES 2 freezer meals, 12 servings each

For years I made only vegetarian lasagna. Meat seemed unnecessary because the vegetables were so tasty. This recipe uses less red sauce than the classic version because the vegetables themselves add moisture. — LA

1 In a large bowl, mix cottage cheese, eggs, and 2 cups Parmesan.

2 Lay baking dishes before you and spread ½ cup red sauce in bottom of each.

3 Assemble both lasagnas at once in layers in the following order:

Layer 1
- 3 uncooked noodles
- 1½ cups red sauce
- 1 cup vegetables
- 1½ cups cottage cheese mixture
- 1 cup mozzarella

Layer 2
- 3 uncooked noodles
- 1½ cups red sauce
- 1 cup vegetables — or whatever remains
- 1½ cups cottage cheese mixture — or whatever remains
- 1 cup mozzarella

Layer 3
- 3 uncooked noodles
- 2 cups red sauce — or whatever remains
- 2 cups mozzarella
- ½ cup Parmesan

4 Wrap each dish entirely in plastic wrap. Top with foil, label, and freeze. Food will stay at optimal quality for up to 2 months in freezer.

TO COOK ONE FREEZER MEAL

1 Thaw one freezer meal in refrigerator or bake it straight from freezer.

2 Preheat oven to 375°F (190°C).

3 Remove foil and plastic wrap from baking dish and replace foil. Place dish on a rimmed baking sheet and bake for 1½ hours if thawed, 2 hours if frozen. Remove foil and continue baking for about 20 minutes, or until lasagna is bubbling and cheese is browned. Remove from oven and let stand 10 minutes before slicing and serving.

INGREDIENTS

- 1 (48-ounce) container cottage cheese (6 cups)
- 4 eggs, lightly beaten
- 3 cups shredded Parmesan cheese (about 12 ounces)
- 11 cups Basic Red Sauce (page 189)
- 18 regular lasagna noodles, uncooked
- 4 cups assorted vegetables in bite-size pieces (mushrooms, zucchini, carrots, onions, green and red bell peppers are nice)
- 8 cups shredded mozzarella cheese (about 2 pounds)

PACK IT UP

Two 13- by 9- by 2-inch baking dishes

Plastic wrap

Aluminum foil

VEGETABLE LASAGNA
SMALL PAN

MAKES 4 freezer meals, 4–6 servings each

INGREDIENTS

1 (48-ounce) container cottage cheese (6 cups)

4 eggs, lightly beaten

3 cups shredded Parmesan cheese (about 12 ounces)

11 cups Basic Red Sauce (page 189)

24 regular lasagna noodles, uncooked

4 cups assorted vegetables in bite-size pieces (mushrooms, zucchini, carrots, onions, green and red bell peppers are nice)

8 cups shredded mozzarella cheese (about 2 pounds)

I like to keep these on hand to serve as a vegetarian option when I need it for guests. — LA

1 In a large bowl, mix cottage cheese, eggs, and 2 cups Parmesan.

2 Lay baking dishes before you and spread ¼ cup red sauce in bottom of each.

3 Assemble all four lasagnas at once in layers in the following order:

Layer 1	Layer 2	Layer 3
• 2 uncooked noodles	• 2 uncooked noodles	• 2 uncooked noodles
• ¾ cup red sauce	• ¾ cup red sauce	• 1 cup red sauce — or whatever remains
• ½ cup vegetables	• ½ cup vegetables — or whatever remains	• 1 cup mozzarella
• ¾ cup cottage cheese mixture	• ¾ cup cottage cheese mixture — or whatever remains	• ¼ cup Parmesan
• ½ cup mozzarella	• ½ cup mozzarella	

4 Wrap each pan entirely in plastic wrap. Top with foil, label, and freeze. Food will stay at optimal quality for up to 2 months in freezer.

TO COOK ONE FREEZER MEAL

1 Thaw one freezer meal in refrigerator or bake it straight from freezer.

2 Preheat oven to 375°F (190°C).

3 Remove foil and plastic wrap from baking dish and replace foil. Bake for 45 minutes if thawed, 1 hour if frozen. Remove foil and continue baking until lasagna is bubbling and cheese is browned. Remove from oven and let stand 10 minutes before slicing and serving.

PACK IT UP

Four 12½- by 6½- by 3-inch foil loaf pans (also known as 5-pound loaf pans or ⅓ size steam table pans)

Plastic wrap

Aluminum foil

APPLES AND CHEDDAR
WITH PECAN CRUMBLE

MAKES 3 freezer side dishes, 8 servings each

This is perfect as a side with pork or chicken dishes. It also serves as a dessert when you want something that isn't very sweet. And it's gluten-free. — LA

1 Divide apples and cheese among three unlabeled 1-gallon freezer bags. Into each bag, measure 1 cup heavy cream and ½ teaspoon salt. Seal bags.

2 Into each sandwich bag, measure 1 cup pecan halves, 2 tablespoons sugar, and 1 teaspoon butter. Seal bags.

3 Into each labeled 1-gallon freezer bag, place one bag apple mixture and one bag pecan mixture.

4 Seal and freeze. Food will stay at optimal quality for up to 2 months in freezer.

TO COOK ONE FREEZER SIDE DISH

1 Completely thaw one freezer side dish in refrigerator.

2 Preheat oven to 350°F (180°C).

3 Put apple mixture in an ungreased baking dish and cover tightly with foil. Bake for 45 minutes. Remove foil and continue baking until apples are soft and sauce is reduced and bubbly.

4 Meanwhile, in a small skillet, mix pecan mixture with 1 tablespoon water. Cook, stirring, over medium heat until pecans and sauce caramelize, about 5 minutes. Remove from heat. Cool and crumble over baked apples.

INGREDIENTS

- 5 pounds tart apples, peeled, cored, and sliced
- 1 pound sharp cheddar cheese, shredded
- 3 cups heavy cream
- 1½ teaspoons salt
- 3 cups (12 ounces) pecan halves (12 ounces)
- 6 tablespoons firmly packed brown sugar
- 3 teaspoons butter

ON HAND FOR COOKING EACH FREEZER SIDE DISH

Aluminum foil

PACK IT UP

Six 1-gallon freezer bags; label 3

Three sandwich bags

CREAM OF ASPARAGUS SOUP

MAKES 3 freezer meals, 4 servings each

Make this soup when fresh asparagus is abundant. This recipe yields fewer servings than most of our other recipes. Feel free to multiply the ingredients, but take care with the seasonings — see our advice about adapting recipes on page 234. — LA

INGREDIENTS

- 2 pounds fresh asparagus, cleaned and fibrous ends snapped off
- 4 cups chicken broth
- ¼ cup chopped onion
- 1 large carrot, cut into 2-inch pieces
- 1 cup heavy cream
- 1 teaspoon salt
- 1 teaspoon black pepper

1 Place asparagus in a large shallow pan with just enough water to cover. Bring to a boil. Reduce heat and simmer for 4 minutes. Drain water, reserving 1 cup. Cut asparagus into 2-inch pieces and set aside.

2 Return reserved water to pan. Add broth, onion, and carrot, and simmer until vegetables are soft, about 10 minutes.

3 In a blender or food processor, combine broth, vegetables, and asparagus until smooth (some small chunks of asparagus are okay). Stir in cream, salt, and pepper. Cool.

4 Divide cooled soup evenly among freezer bags.

5 Seal and freeze. Food will stay at optimal quality for up to 2 months in freezer.

PACK IT UP

Three 1-quart freezer bags, labeled

TO COOK ONE FREEZER MEAL

1 Completely thaw one bag in refrigerator.

2 In a medium saucepan, reheat soup over low heat.

GARLIC MASHED POTATOES

MAKES 4 freezer side dishes, 6 servings each

Not only is it convenient to have a main dish prepared ahead of time, but it can be equally satisfying to serve a side dish with no extra fuss at dinnertime. — LA

INGREDIENTS

10	pounds russet potatoes, peeled and cut into large chunks
1	tablespoon olive oil
2	tablespoons minced garlic
2	(8-ounce) packages cream cheese, cut into quarters
1	teaspoon salt
1	teaspoon black pepper
1	cup chicken broth

1 Put potatoes in a large stockpot with water to cover. Bring to a boil and cook potatoes until they break apart easily with a fork, 9 to 12 minutes.

2 Meanwhile, in a small skillet, heat oil over medium heat. Add garlic and cook, stirring occasionally, until soft, about 3 minutes. Remove pan from heat.

3 Drain potatoes and return them to pot. Add garlic with oil, cream cheese, salt, and pepper; mash potatoes. Stir in broth. Divide potatoes evenly among baking dishes. Wrap each dish entirely in plastic wrap and cover with foil.

4 Label and freeze. Food will stay at optimal quality for up to 2 months in freezer.

TO COOK ONE FREEZER SIDE DISH

1 Thaw one freezer side dish in refrigerator or bake straight from freezer.

2 Preheat oven to 350°F (180°C).

3 Remove foil and plastic wrap from baking dish and replace foil. Bake for 1 hour if frozen, 30 minutes if thawed, or until potatoes are hot all the way through.

PACK IT UP

Four 8-inch square baking dishes

Plastic wrap

Aluminum foil

BAKED POTATO CHOWDER

MAKES 4 freezer meals, 6 servings each

This hearty soup is filling enough for dinner but makes a great quick lunch, too. Package in some 1-gallon bags and some in 1-quart bags for the most flexibility. — LA

1 Cut potatoes in half; scoop out flesh. Set potato aside and discard skins, or save for another use (see box below).

2 In a large stockpot, melt butter over medium heat. Add onion and cook, stirring, until soft, about 5 minutes. Add parsley, beef base, basil, garlic, salt, and pepper; cook, stirring, for 2 minutes. Add flour; cook, stirring, for 2 minutes longer. Mixture will be like a paste. Gradually add water, half-and-half, and potato, and cook, stirring frequently, until soup has thickened, about 30 minutes. Add cheese and stir until melted. Cool.

3 Divide cooled soup evenly among freezer bags. Seal and freeze. Food will stay at optimal quality for up to 2 months in freezer.

TO COOK ONE FREEZER MEAL

1 Completely thaw one freezer meal in refrigerator.

2 In a large saucepan, bring soup to a simmer over medium heat. Do not boil.

INGREDIENTS

- 10 pounds russet potatoes, baked and cooled
- 1 cup (2 sticks) butter
- 2 cups chopped onion (about 2 medium)
- ¼ cup dried parsley
- 2 tablespoons beef base
- 1 tablespoon dried basil
- 1 tablespoon minced garlic
- 2 teaspoons salt
- 2 teaspoons black pepper
- 2 cups all-purpose flour
- 12 cups water
- 4 cups half-and-half or light cream
- 1 pound sharp cheddar cheese, cut into large chunks

PACK IT UP
Four 1-gallon freezer bags, labeled

SAVE THOSE SKINS!

Potato skins make a fun snack. Sprinkle with dried or fresh herbs, crumbled bacon, and shredded cheese. Broil in the oven until cheese melts. Serve with sour cream or guacamole. Or just spread them with a bit of butter and sprinkle with salt and pepper. Yum!

BLACK BEAN SOUP

MAKES 3 freezer meals, 6–8 servings each

This hearty and healthy dairy-free, gluten-free soup can be made vegan by replacing the chicken broth with vegetable stock. If you'll also be serving meat eaters, pass shredded cooked chicken at the table. Use our method on page 65 for cooking whole chicken or, if pressed for time, use a rotisserie chicken from the grocery store deli. — LA

NOTE: If you are using dried black beans, it is not necessary to soak them before cooking. In a large pot, add 3 pounds dried black beans and enough water to cover by about 3 inches. Bring to a boil, reduce heat to a simmer, and cook until beans are soft to your liking, about 1½ hours. Add water if necessary to keep beans covered. Drain and use beans in the recipe.

1 In a large pot, heat oil over medium heat. Add onion, jalapeño, garlic, salt, black pepper, coriander, oregano, turmeric, and paprika, and cook, stirring, until onion is soft and spices are fragrant, about 10 minutes. Remove from heat and stir in carrots and cilantro. Cool.

2 Divide cooled vegetable mixture evenly among freezer bags. Divide beans evenly over vegetables. Into each bag, add 3 cups chicken or vegetable broth, 1 can tomatoes, and 2 tablespoons lime juice.

3 Seal and freeze. Food will stay at optimal quality for up to 3 months in freezer.

TO COOK ONE FREEZER MEAL

Stovetop
In a large pan, simmer frozen or thawed soup over medium heat until vegetables are tender, about 30 minutes.

Slow Cooker
Cook frozen or thawed soup until vegetables are tender, 8 hours on low or 4 hours on high.

INGREDIENTS

- ¼ cup olive oil
- 6 cups chopped onion (about 3 large)
- 6 tablespoons minced jalapeño (about 3 large)
- 3 tablespoons minced garlic
- 3 teaspoons salt
- 3 teaspoons black pepper
- 1½ teaspoons coriander
- 1½ teaspoons oregano
- 1 teaspoon ground turmeric
- 1 teaspoon smoked paprika
- 6 cups chopped carrots (about 12 medium)
- 3 cups chopped loosely packed cilantro
- 12 (15-oz) cans black beans, drained and rinsed, or 3 pounds (6 cups) dried beans (see Note)
- 9 cups chicken or vegetable broth
- 3 (14.5-ounce) cans diced tomatoes
- 6 tablespoons lime juice

PACK IT UP
Three 1-gallon freezer bags, labeled

BLACK BEAN
AND VEGETABLE CHILI

MAKES 4 freezer meals, 8 servings each

INGREDIENTS

1 pound fresh white mush-rooms, cleaned and sliced

6 cups sliced carrots (about 12 medium)

6 cups sliced celery (about 12 stalks)

4 cups chopped onion (about 4 medium)

2 large green bell peppers, cut into 1-inch pieces

12 cups Basic Red Sauce (page 189)

8 (15-ounce) cans kidney beans, drained and rinsed if you prefer

4 (15-ounce) cans black beans, drained and rinsed if you prefer

4 tablespoons chili powder

4 tablespoons hot pepper sauce

4 teaspoons minced garlic

4 teaspoons dried oregano

4 teaspoons black pepper

This is a delicious and easy-to-make variation on our Classic Chili (page 92). When I know I'll be feeding a mixed crowd of vegetarians and meat eaters, I simply give guests a choice between the two. — LA

1 Into each freezer bag measure one-quarter of mushrooms, 1½ cups carrots, 1½ cups celery, 1 cup onion, one-quarter of bell peppers, 3 cups red sauce, 2 cans kidney beans, 1 can black beans, 1 tablespoon chili powder, 1 tablespoon hot pepper sauce, 1 teaspoon garlic, 1 teaspoon oregano, and 1 teaspoon black pepper.

2 Seal and freeze. Food will stay at optimal quality for up to 3 months in freezer.

TO COOK ONE FREEZER MEAL

1 Completely thaw one freezer meal in refrigerator.

2 In a medium saucepan, cook chili over medium-low heat until liquid cooks off and chili is thick, about 1 hour.

PACK IT UP
Four 1-gallon freezer bags, labeled

CREAM OF MUSHROOM SOUP

MAKES 3 freezer meals, 4 servings each

This soup is ideal for lunch. Forget canned and condensed — make the real thing for yourself and taste the difference. — LA

1 In a large stockpot, melt butter over medium heat. Add mushrooms and cook, stirring, until soft, about 10 minutes. Add flour and cook, stirring, for 2 minutes. Add broth, salt, and pepper; cook, stirring, until soup is smooth and has thickened, about 5 minutes. Stir in cream. Cool.

2 Divide cooled soup evenly among freezer bags.

3 Seal and freeze. Food will stay at optimal quality for up to 2 months in freezer.

TO COOK ONE FREEZER MEAL

1 Completely thaw one bag in refrigerator.

2 In a medium saucepan, reheat soup over low heat.

INGREDIENTS

- ½ cup (1 stick) butter
- 2½ pounds fresh white mushrooms, cleaned and sliced
- ½ cup all-purpose flour
- 4 cups chicken broth
- 1 teaspoon salt
- 1 teaspoon black pepper
- 2 cups heavy cream

PACK IT UP
Three 1-quart freezer bags, labeled

CHICKEN BROTH IN A VEGETABLE SOUP?

We love the flavor of chicken broth, but you can make this or any of our other meatless soups vegetarian by substituting vegetable broth for the chicken or beef broth.

SEAFOOD CREOLE

MAKES 3 freezer meals, 6–8 servings each

INGREDIENTS

- 3 (46-ounce) cans/bottles vegetable juice (such as V8)
- 3 large green bell peppers, diced
- 3 large celery stalks, diced
- 3 large onions, diced
- 3 tablespoons minced garlic
- 3 teaspoons paprika
- 3 teaspoons salt
- 3 teaspoons black pepper
- 3 teaspoons dried parsley
- ¾ teaspoon celery seed
- ¾ teaspoon cayenne pepper
- 4½ pounds bite-size pieces of seafood in any combination (shrimp, scallops, crabmeat, halibut, cod)

I took an old family recipe and enlivened it. If you love seafood, you'll love this simple supper. Serve over rice. — LA

1 Using a large, sturdy container to hold the bag (see page 15 for method), carefully pour 1 container of vegetable juice into each unlabeled 1-gallon freezer bag. Divide bell peppers, celery, and onions evenly among bags of juice. Into each bag, measure 1 tablespoon garlic, 1 teaspoon paprika, 1 teaspoon salt, 1 teaspoon black pepper, 1 teaspoon parsley, ¼ teaspoon celery seed, and ¼ teaspoon cayenne. Seal bags.

2 Into each 1-quart freezer bag, measure 1½ pounds seafood. Place a bag of vegetable juice mixture and a bag of seafood into each labeled 1-gallon bag.

3 Seal and freeze. Food will stay at optimal quality for up to 2 months in freezer.

TO COOK ONE FREEZER MEAL

1 Completely thaw one freezer meal in refrigerator.

2 In a large stockpot, bring vegetable mixture to a boil. Reduce heat and simmer for 20 minutes. Add seafood and continue to simmer gently until seafood is thoroughly cooked, 5 to 7 minutes.

PACK IT UP

Six 1-gallon freezer bags; label 3

Three 1-quart bags

TOMATO-BASIL SOUP

MAKES 3 freezer meals, 4 servings each

INGREDIENTS

- ½ cup (1 stick) butter
- 3 cups chopped onion (about 3 medium)
- 1 teaspoon minced garlic
- 3 pounds Roma tomatoes, chopped
- 8 cups chicken broth
- 1 tablespoon lime juice
- Pinch of sugar
- ¾ cup chopped fresh basil leaves
- Zest of 1 orange

PACK IT UP

Three 1-gallon freezer bags, labeled

The flavor of this tomato soup is unique, I found, and I wanted to be sure to share it with our readers. We've made only minor changes to Carol Costenbader's original recipe in *The Big Book of Preserving the Harvest*. Enjoy! — KN

1 In a stockpot, melt butter over low heat. Add onion and cook, stirring, until soft, about 15 minutes. Add garlic and cook, stirring, for 2 minutes. Add tomatoes, broth, lime juice, and sugar; bring to a boil. Reduce heat and simmer, covered, for 15 minutes. Stir in basil and orange zest.

2 Let soup cool slightly, then transfer to a food processor and purée. Cool completely. Divide cooled soup evenly among freezer bags.

3 Seal and freeze. Food will stay at optimal quality for up to 4 months in freezer.

TO COOK ONE FREEZER MEAL

1 Completely thaw one freezer meal in refrigerator.

2 In a medium saucepan, reheat soup over medium-low heat.

FRENCH ONION SOUP

MAKES 5 freezer meals, 4 servings each

If you're an onion lover, this soup is for you. I like to freeze this in complete packages: soup, bread, and cheese. That way, I don't need to have anything particular on hand when I want to serve it. — LA

1 Place onion halves cut side down on a cutting board and slice into ½-inch strips.

2 In a large stockpot, heat oil and butter over medium heat. Add onions and salt. Cook, stirring frequently, for 1 hour. Reduce heat if onions begin to get too brown. Add sherry, beef base, Worcestershire, garlic, and pepper, and cook, stirring to loosen any bits of onion on bottom of pot, for about 10 minutes. Cool.

3 Divide cooled onion mixture among unlabeled 1-gallon freezer bags. Seal bags.

4 Into each sandwich bag measure 1 cup cheese. Seal bags.

5 Into each labeled 1-gallon freezer bag place one bag of onion mixture, one bag of cheese, and 4 slices of bread.

6 Seal and freeze. Food will stay at optimal quality for up to 4 months in freezer.

TO COOK ONE FREEZER MEAL

1 Completely thaw one freezer meal in refrigerator.

2 Preheat oven broiler.

3 Place four ovenproof bowls on a rimmed baking sheet and divide onion mixture among them. Add 1 cup boiling water to each bowl. Toast bread slices and put 1 piece on top of each bowl of soup. Divide cheese evenly over bread slices. Broil just until cheese melts and browns. Take care when serving the soup: Bowls will be very hot.

INGREDIENTS

- 10 pounds onions, peeled and cut in half
- ½ cup olive oil
- ½ cup (1 stick) butter
- 1 tablespoon salt
- ½ cup cooking sherry
- 2 tablespoons beef base
- 2 tablespoons Worcestershire sauce
- 1 tablespoon minced garlic
- 1 tablespoon black pepper
- 5 cups shredded Swiss or Gouda cheese (about 1¼ pounds)
- 20 small slices French bread

ON HAND FOR COOKING EACH FREEZER MEAL

- 4 cups boiling water

PACK IT UP
Ten 1-gallon freezer bags; label 5

Five sandwich bags

SAUCES, MARINADES,
AND FLAVORED BUTTERS

ASIAN MARKET MARINADE

MAKES 2 freezer marinades

INGREDIENTS

- 1 cup Asian-style salad dressing (such as Newman's Own Sesame Ginger)
- ½ cup peanut sauce
- ¼ cup reduced-sodium soy sauce
- 4 teaspoons toasted sesame oil
- ½ teaspoon red curry paste or hot chili oil
- 4 tablespoons chopped scallions

All of my testers for this recipe were impressed by the flavors in the simple, versatile marinade. Use one marinade for Portobello Mushrooms (page 181) or Fresh Vegetable Stir-Fry (page 182). — KN

1 In a small bowl, whisk together salad dressing, peanut sauce, soy sauce, oil, and curry paste. Divide sauce evenly between freezer containers. Into each container, measure 2 tablespoons scallions.

2 Seal and freeze. Food will stay at optimal quality for up to 3 months in freezer.

PACK IT UP
Two small square freezer containers, labeled

PORTOBELLO MUSHROOMS
WITH ASIAN MARKET MARINADE

MAKES 2 servings

One container of sauce is appropriate for two grilled mushrooms, which, divided, are a perfect lunch for four. For a dinner entrée, use both containers to marinate four mushroom caps. Serve over rice or noodles. — KN

1 Completely thaw marinade in refrigerator.

2 Gently stir to recombine, and marinate mushroom caps for 1 hour.

3 Prepare a medium-low fire in a gas or charcoal grill.

4 Grill for 6 to 8 minutes per side, or until tender. Slice and serve. Garnish with scallions, peanuts, or cilantro, if desired.

PREP AHEAD

1 container Asian Market Marinade (page 180)

INGREDIENTS

2 portobello mushroom caps, cleaned

Chopped scallions, chopped peanuts, or chopped fresh cilantro, for garnish (optional)

FRESH VEGETABLE STIR-FRY
WITH ASIAN MARINATED TOFU

MAKES 6–8 servings

PREP AHEAD

1 container Asian Market Marinade (page 180)

INGREDIENTS

1 pound extra-firm tofu, cut into 1-inch pieces

1 teaspoon sesame oil

2 cups broccoli florets (about 5 ounces)

1 cup green beans, cut into 1-inch pieces (about 4 ounces)

1 cup chopped scallions (about 6)

1 cup sliced carrots (about 2 medium)

5 ounces soba noodles, cooked and drained

½ cup roasted peanuts, chopped (optional)

This dish is full of fiber plus important vitamins and minerals such as vitamin A, vitamin C, potassium, and folic acid. Many of the vegetables are available at farmers' markets during the growing season. Farmers' markets are fun for the whole family and a great way to support your local growers. If your family doesn't like tofu, omit it and enjoy the vegetables and Asian flavors. — KN

1 Completely thaw marinade in refrigerator.

2 Gently stir marinade to recombine and set aside ¼ cup.

3 In a medium bowl, mix tofu with remaining marinade to coat. Marinate in refrigerator for 1 to 2 hours, stirring occasionally. Drain marinade from tofu.

4 In a wok, heat oil over medium-high heat. Add tofu and cook, stirring, until lightly browned, 4 to 5 minutes. Add broccoli, green beans, scallions, and carrots. Cook, stirring, until vegetables are tender crisp, 4 to 5 minutes. Add reserved marinade and noodles, and cook until heated through.

5 Garnish with peanuts, if desired.

LEMONY
CAESAR MARINADE

MAKES 2 freezer marinades, ¾ cup each

INGREDIENTS

- ¾ cup olive oil
- ¼ cup lemon juice
- ¼ cup white wine vinegar
- 2 teaspoons Dijon mustard
- ½ teaspoon salt
- 2 teaspoons minced garlic
- ½ teaspoon black pepper

This lemony marinade is reminiscent of a Caesar dressing. Unlike the creamy versions found commercially, this is lighter and tangier. — LA

1 In a small bowl, whisk together oil, lemon juice, vinegar, mustard, and salt. Divide marinade evenly between freezer containers. Into each container, measure 1 teaspoon garlic and ¼ teaspoon pepper.

2 Seal and gently shake each container to combine contents. Freeze. Food will stay at optimal quality for up to 3 months in freezer.

PACK IT UP

*Two small freezer containers,
labeled*

PORTOBELLO MUSHROOMS

Portobellos are a perfect meat substitute. They're sometimes referred to as steak mushrooms because of their size and suitability for marinating and grilling.

LEMONY CAESAR
PORTOBELLO MUSHROOMS

MAKES 2 servings

One of my favorite ways to enjoy a salad is with hot, cooked mushrooms. Use some of the marinade as a dressing for romaine lettuce and top with these marinated and grilled portobellos and some crispy homemade croutons. — LA

1 Completely thaw marinade in refrigerator.

2 In a bowl, marinate mushroom caps for 1 hour.

3 For outdoor cooking: Prepare a medium fire in a gas or charcoal grill. Grill mushrooms, turning occasionally, for 10 to 12 minutes, or until tender. Stuff each mushroom cap with 2 tablespoons Parmesan and grill until melted.

4 For indoor cooking: Arrange mushrooms on an ungreased broiler pan. Broil under high heat, 5 inches from heat source, for about 2 minutes on each side. Stuff each mushroom cap with 2 tablespoons Parmesan and broil until melted.

PREP AHEAD

1   container Lemony Caesar Marinade (page 184)

INGREDIENTS

2   portobello mushroom caps, cleaned

¼   cup shredded Parmesan cheese (about 1 ounce)

OLIVE OIL

Products carrying a store's brand label are developing a positive reputation as quality products offered at a lower price than name brands. For example, my wholesale club's store brand extra-virgin olive oil is two to three times less expensive per ounce than even the least expensive brand at the grocery store. Extra-virgin olive oil is from the first pressing of olives and is the finest olive oil one can buy. Keep your bottle tightly sealed and stored away from heat and light.

MAPLE MARINADE

MAKES 2 freezer marinades, about ¾ cup each

This marinade, with the subtle sweetness of maple syrup, is well suited for vegetables. — LA

1 In a medium bowl, whisk together maple syrup, oil, lemon juice, mustard, and salt. Divide marinade evenly between freezer containers. Into each container, measure 2 teaspoons garlic, ½ teaspoon thyme, and ½ teaspoon pepper.

2 Seal and gently shake each container to combine contents. Freeze. Food will stay at optimal quality for up to 3 months in freezer.

INGREDIENTS

- ½ cup maple syrup
- ½ cup olive oil
- ¼ cup lemon juice
- 2 tablespoons spicy brown mustard
- 1 teaspoon salt
- 4 teaspoons minced garlic
- 1 teaspoon dried thyme
- 1 teaspoon black pepper

PACK IT UP
Two small square freezer containers, labeled

FEAST TONIGHT

MAPLE
PORTOBELLO MUSHROOMS

MAKES 2 servings

These grilled mushrooms team up nicely with polenta, couscous, or quinoa. — LA

1 Completely thaw marinade in refrigerator.

2 In a bowl, marinate mushroom caps for 1 hour.

3 For outdoor cooking: Prepare a medium fire in a gas or charcoal grill. Grill mushrooms, turning occasionally, for 10 to 12 minutes, or until tender.

4 For indoor cooking: Arrange mushrooms on a greased broiler pan. Broil under high heat, 5 inches from heat source, for about 2 minutes on each side.

PREP AHEAD

- 1 container Maple Marinade (above)

INGREDIENTS

- 2 portobello mushroom caps, cleaned

CHIPOTLE-ROASTED
TOMATO SAUCE

MAKES 7–10 cups

INGREDIENTS

7½–9   pounds fresh Roma
        tomatoes

½   teaspoon salt (optional)

6   chipotle peppers in adobo
        sauce, halved and seeded

1½   pounds onions, sliced

1½   teaspoons vegetable oil

PACK IT UP
Seven 1-pint freezer bags, labeled

This sauce is excellent with cheese ravioli and other pasta dishes. You will also find it in Cinco-Layer Bake (page 59) and the Tex-Mex variation of Cajun Braised Skillet Chops (page 116). — KN

1 Preheat oven to 475°F (245°C).

2 Rinse and slice tomatoes in half lengthwise. Arrange in a single layer in several baking dishes. Sprinkle salt, if using, over tomatoes. Add chipotle peppers and onions to each baking dish; mix to combine. Drizzle oil over vegetable mixture. Bake for 30 to 35 minutes, or until tomatoes are soft and onions are beginning to brown.

3 Cool tomatoes enough to handle. Slide skins off. Remove chipotle peppers and discard.

4 Using a food processor and working in batches, spoon tomatoes and onions into processor's bowl with a slotted spoon so that juice can drain back into dish. Purée tomatoes and onions until smooth. Add juices from baking dish if sauce is too thick. Discard remaining juice.

5 Divide sauce among freezer bags.

6 Seal and freeze. Food will stay at optimal quality for up to 6 months in freezer.

TO ENJOY

1 Completely thaw one bag in refrigerator.

2 Use in a recipe calling for tomato sauce for a chipotle-enlivened dish, or simmer in a medium saucepan over medium-low heat for 5 to 10 minutes and pour over your favorite pasta.

BASIC RED SAUCE
LARGE BATCH

MAKES about 40 cups, or 10 quarts, or 2½ gallons

This simple sauce is not cooked before it's frozen. Six to eight cups is a good amount to package for a meal for four to six people. It can be hard to envision the yield of 10 quarts — if you aren't sure your pot is big enough before you start, check by measuring an equivalent amount of water. If you need to, divide this recipe between two large pots or large bowls. — LA

NOTE: Use half of the tomato paste for this recipe and freeze the other half in a freezer container or freezer bag to use next time you make this sauce.

1 In a large stockpot, mix tomato paste and hot water until smooth. Stir in onion, parsley, garlic, sugar, salt, basil, oregano, and thyme.

2 Add tomato sauce and diced tomatoes, and mix well. Do not cook.

3 Measure sauce into appropriate portions for immediate use. Divide remaining sauce evenly among 1-gallon freezer bags for later use.

4 Seal and label each bag with amount of sauce inside. Freeze. Food will stay at optimal quality for up to 6 months in freezer.

TO ENJOY

1 Completely thaw one bag in refrigerator.

2 Use in a recipe calling for tomato sauce, or simmer in a saucepan over medium-low heat for 20 minutes and pour over your favorite pasta.

3 To use in a meat sauce, brown and drain 1 pound lean ground beef for every 8 cups of sauce; add cooked beef to sauce and gently reheat.

INGREDIENTS

- 1 (111-ounce) can tomato paste, halved (see Note), or 4 (12-ounce) cans
- 8 cups hot water
- ½ cup minced onion
- ½ cup dried parsley
- ¼ cup minced garlic
- ¼ cup sugar
- 2 tablespoons salt
- 2 teaspoons dried basil
- 2 teaspoons dried oregano
- 2 teaspoons dried thyme
- 1 (106-ounce) can tomato sauce or 4 (28-ounce) cans
- 1 (102-ounce) can diced tomatoes or 4 (28-ounce) cans

PACK IT UP
Several 1-gallon freezer bags (number will vary)

BASIC RED SAUCE
SMALL BATCH

MAKES about 10 cups

INGREDIENTS

- 1 (12-ounce) can tomato paste
- 2 cups hot water
- 2 tablespoons minced onion
- 2 tablespoons dried parsley
- 1 tablespoon minced garlic
- 1 tablespoon sugar
- 2 teaspoons salt
- ½ teaspoon dried basil
- ½ teaspoon dried oregano
- ½ teaspoon dried thyme
- 1 (28-ounce) can tomato sauce
- 1 (28-ounce) can diced tomatoes

This all-purpose tomato sauce can be used anywhere a red sauce or marinara sauce is needed. — LA

---

1 In a large bowl, mix tomato paste and hot water until smooth. Stir in onion, parsley, garlic, sugar, salt, basil, oregano, and thyme.

2 Add tomato sauce and diced tomatoes, and mix well. Do not cook.

3 Measure sauce into appropriate portions for immediate use. Divide remaining sauce evenly among 1-quart freezer bags for later use.

4 Seal and label each bag with amount of sauce inside. Freeze. Food will stay at optimal quality for up to 6 months in freezer.

TO ENJOY

1 Completely thaw one bag in refrigerator.

2 Use in a recipe calling for tomato sauce, or simmer in a saucepan over medium-low heat for 20 minutes and pour over your favorite pasta.

3 To use in a meat sauce, brown and drain 1 pound lean ground beef for every 8 cups of sauce; add cooked beef to sauce and gently reheat.

PACK IT UP

*Several 1-quart freezer bags
(number will vary)*

RECIPE SUGGESTIONS FOR BASIC RED SAUCE

Basic Red Sauce is a true staple in our freezers. You will find it in:

Beef-Barley Soup (page 104)

Black Bean and Vegetable Chili (page 172)

Chicken Parmigiana (page 26)

Classic Chili (page 92)

Classic Lasagna (page 79)

Feta and Spinach Lasagna Rolls (page 151)

Manicotti (page 162)

Pork Loin Ragout (page 130)

Pork Ragout Lasagna (page 132)

Spanish Rice (page 78)

Vegetable Lasagna (page 163)

MAMA'S PIZZA SAUCE

MAKES about 10 cups (enough for about ten 16-inch pizzas)

INGREDIENTS

- 1 (106-ounce) can tomato sauce or 4 (28-ounce) cans
- 4 (6-ounce) cans tomato paste
- 1 tablespoon basil
- 1 tablespoon oregano
- 1 teaspoon black pepper
- ½ teaspoon red pepper flakes
- 1 medium onion, peeled and cut in half
- 6 large garlic cloves, peeled and cut in half
- 1 medium stalk celery, cut in half
- 2 bay leaves

PACK IT UP

Ten 1-pint freezer bags, labeled

This recipe is delicious, easy to make, and saves me oodles of money. When I discovered that most of the small jars of pizza sauce cost more than one of those #10 cans of tomato sauce, I got busy developing my own recipe! Take note: This recipe works best in 6-quart (or larger) slow cookers. — KN

---

1 In a slow cooker, combine tomato sauce and tomato paste. Mix until smooth.

2 Stir in basil, oregano, black pepper, and red pepper flakes. Add onion, garlic, celery, and bay leaves.

3 Cook on low, with lid cracked, for 4 to 6 hours. Stir occasionally.

4 Remove onion, garlic, celery, and bay leaves and discard. Divide remaining sauce evenly among 1-pint freezer bags for later use.

5 Seal and freeze. Food will stay at optimal quality for up to 6 months in freezer.

TO THAW

1 Completely thaw one portion in refrigerator. Or place frozen sauce in a small saucepan and heat until able to spread.

BROWN SUGAR AND BOURBON
MARINADE

MAKES 2 freezer marinades

This marinade is excellent for summer grilling your choice of meat or with Bourbon-Marinated Salmon (below). — KN

1 In a large bowl, whisk together orange juice, sugar, bourbon, and soy sauce. Divide evenly between freezer containers.

2 Into each container, measure 2 tablespoons onion and 1 teaspoon garlic. Divide the ginger slices evenly between containers.

3 Seal and gently shake each container to combine contents. Freeze. Food will stay at optimal quality for up to 3 months in freezer.

INGREDIENTS

- 2 cups orange juice
- 1 cup firmly packed brown sugar
- ½ cup bourbon
- ½ cup soy sauce
- 4 tablespoons diced onion
- 2 teaspoons minced garlic
- 2 ounces ginger (about 2½-inch piece), peeled and cut into ⅛-inch-thick slices

PACK IT UP
Two medium square freezer containers, labeled

FEAST TONIGHT

BOURBON-MARINATED SALMON

MAKES 4 servings

This salmon is very nice served with sweet potatoes or fresh fruit salad. — KN

1 Completely thaw marinade in refrigerator.

2 Place 2 pounds salmon in an ungreased 13- by 9-inch baking dish. Pour marinade over salmon and marinate for 6 to 8 hours in refrigerator.

3 Prepare a medium fire in a gas or charcoal grill.

4 Grill salmon, turning occasionally, for 10 to 15 minutes, or until fish flakes easily with a fork. Discard remaining marinade.

PREP AHEAD

- 1 Brown Sugar and Bourbon Marinade (above)

INGREDIENTS

- 2 pounds salmon

GORGONZOLA-PECAN BUTTER

MAKES 4 butter logs, about ⅓ cup each

This compound butter offers a great way to use up pecans left over from holiday baking. I wrote this recipe to yield an ample amount for those large holiday gatherings of friends and family. — KN

INGREDIENTS

- 1 cup (2 sticks) unsalted butter, softened
- ⅔ cup (3.5 ounces) finely crumbled Gorgonzola cheese
- 2 tablespoons pecans, finely chopped

1 In a medium bowl, mix butter, Gorgonzola, and pecans.

2 Divide mixture into quarters and place each portion on a sheet of waxed paper. Roll paper tightly so that butter is shaped like a log; place all four butter logs in freezer bag.

3 Seal and freeze. Butter will stay at optimal quality for up to 2 months in freezer and in an airtight container in refrigerator for up to 2 weeks.

TO ENJOY
Completely thaw one butter log in refrigerator.

PACK IT UP
Waxed paper

One 1-quart freezer bag, labeled

FEAST TONIGHT

GREEN BEANS
WITH GORGONZOLA-PECAN BUTTER

MAKES 1 side dish, 2 servings

Try this recipe in the summer, when green beans are at their peak. Serve with a simple grilled meat or fish entrée. — KN

PREP AHEAD

- 1 tablespoon Gorgonzola-Pecan Butter (above), or more to taste

INGREDIENTS

- 8 ounces fresh green beans, washed, trimmed, and cut into 2-inch pieces

1 Place 1 tablespoon butter in a small dish and allow it to soften outside of refrigerator as you prepare green beans.

2 Steam green beans until tender crisp.

3 Transfer beans to a medium serving dish and toss with softened butter. Serve immediately.

BUTTERNUT SQUASH
WITH GORGONZOLA-PECAN BUTTER

MAKES 1 side dish, 4 servings

PREP AHEAD

2 tablespoons Gorgonzola-
   Pecan Butter (page 196)

INGREDIENTS

1 medium butternut squash
   (1 pound), peeled and
   cubed

1 tablespoon olive oil

¼ teaspoon salt

Many grocery stores carry precut butternut squash in their produce sections. It's an easy shortcut for busy nights. — KN

1 Preheat oven to 400°F (200°C).

2 Place butter in a small dish and allow it to soften outside of refrigerator as you prepare squash.

3 In a medium bowl, toss butternut squash with oil and salt. Place squash on a rimmed baking sheet and bake for 25 minutes.

4 Transfer cooked squash to a deep serving dish and toss with softened butter. Serve immediately.

WALNUT-PESTO BUTTER

MAKES 2 logs, about ⅔ cup each

This compound butter can spruce up plain seafood, a baked potato, or pasta. Enjoy with Salmon, recipe below. — KN

1 In a small bowl and using a wooden spoon or scraper, blend butter and pesto. Stir in walnuts.

2 Divide mixture in half and place each portion on a sheet of waxed paper. Roll paper tightly so that butter is shaped like a log; place both butter logs in freezer bag. Seal and freeze. Butter will stay at optimal quality for up to 2 months in freezer and in an airtight container in the refrigerator for up to 2 weeks.

TO ENJOY
Completely thaw one butter log in refrigerator.

INGREDIENTS

- 1 cup (2 sticks) butter, softened
- ⅓ cup pesto (try Perfect Pesto on page 207)
- 2 tablespoons finely chopped walnuts

PACK IT UP

Waxed paper

One 1-quart freezer bag, labeled

FEAST TONIGHT

SALMON
WITH WALNUT-PESTO BUTTER

MAKES 4 servings

Both salmon and walnuts are nutritional superstars, because they are high in omega-3 fatty acid. We particularly enjoy this healthful dish during the holidays, when there are extra walnuts from baking projects that need to be used up. Serve with fresh steamed broccoli or a lightly dressed spinach salad. — KN

1 Completely thaw butter log in refrigerator.

2 Prepare a medium fire in a gas or charcoal grill.

3 Cook salmon, turning occasionally, for 10 to 15 minutes, or until fish flakes easily with a fork. Top salmon with butter.

PREP AHEAD

- 1 log Walnut-Pesto Butter (above)

INGREDIENTS

- 2 pounds salmon

GORGONZOLA-
LEMON-PEPPER BUTTER

MAKES 2 butter logs, about ⅓ cup each

Having a main dish finished and in the freezer is like having a basic black dress in the closet. And just as the accessories complete the outfit, having the main dish out of the way means that I can explore new ways to accessorize my meal. Compound butters like this one can be enjoyed tossed with steamed or roasted vegetables or pasta. — KN

1 In a small bowl, blend butter and lemon-pepper salt. Stir in Gorgonzola.

2 Divide mixture in half and place each portion on a sheet of waxed paper.

3 Roll paper tightly so that butter is shaped like a log; place both butter logs in freezer bag.

4 Seal and freeze. Butter will stay at optimal quality for up to 2 months in freezer and in an airtight container in refrigerator for up to 2 weeks.

TO ENJOY
Completely thaw one butter log in refrigerator.

INGREDIENTS

- ½ cup (1 stick) unsalted butter, softened
- 1 tablespoon lemon-pepper seasoning salt
- ⅓ cup finely crumbled Gorgonzola cheese

PACK IT UP
Waxed paper

One 1-quart freezer bag, labeled

SALT-FREE VARIATION

For those interested in eliminating the salt but not the flavor of this butter, in place of the seasoning salt try a salt-free seasoning, such as Penzeys Florida Seasoned Pepper.

LINGUINE WITH ROASTED SWEET POTATO AND GORGONZOLA-LEMON-PEPPER BUTTER

MAKES 4–6 servings

PREP AHEAD

1 log Gorgonzola-Lemon-Pepper Butter (or as much as desired; page 201)

INGREDIENTS

1 pound sweet potatoes or yams, peeled and cubed

2 tablespoons balsamic vinegar

1 pound fresh or dried linguine or your favorite pasta

Roasting vegetables with a splash of balsamic vinegar complements the richness of the Gorgonzola and butter. — LA

1 Preheat oven to 425°F (220°C).

2 Place butter in a small dish and allow it to soften outside of the refrigerator.

3 On a rimmed baking sheet, toss sweet potatoes with balsamic vinegar. Bake for 15 to 20 minutes, or until soft and beginning to brown on edges.

4 Meanwhile, cook pasta according to directions, timing it so pasta is done about the same time as sweet potatoes.

5 In a deep serving dish, toss hot cooked pasta and roasted sweet potatoes with softened butter. Serve immediately.

CHILI-LIME BUTTER

MAKES 2 compound butters, about ¼ cup each

Use this butter to baste shrimp or corn on the cob. — LA

1 In a small bowl, combine butter, oil, chili powder, garlic, oregano, lime juice, soy sauce, and cumin. Divide mixture evenly between freezer containers.

2 Seal and freeze. Butter will stay at optimal quality for up to 2 months in freezer.

INGREDIENTS

- 4 tablespoons butter, softened
- ¼ cup olive oil
- 2 teaspoons chili powder
- 2 teaspoons minced garlic
- 2 teaspoons dried oregano
- 2 tablespoons lime juice
- 2 tablespoons soy sauce
- ½ teaspoon ground cumin

PACK IT UP

Two small square freezer containers, labeled

HALIBUT
WITH CHILI-LIME BUTTER

MAKES 4 servings

PREP AHEAD

1   container Chili-Lime
    Butter (page 203)

INGREDIENTS

2   pounds halibut

Halibut is my favorite fish. A cold-water fish, it has firm flesh and a mild flavor. If you can't find halibut, substitute another white fish such as cod. — LA

1 Completely thaw butter in refrigerator. Grease a baking dish with some of thawed butter.

2 Preheat oven to 400°F (200°C).

3 Place fish in prepared baking dish. Cover with remaining butter and bake, uncovered, for 20 minutes, or until fish is opaque and flakes easily with a fork.

LEFTOVER FISH?

Any leftover baked fish is perfect in fish tacos! Fill warm corn tortillas with Chili-Lime Halibut, shredded napa cabbage, and fresh cilantro. Add a squeeze of fresh lime, a drizzle of salsa, and a dollop of sour cream.

PERFECT PESTO

MAKES 1⅓ cups

Pesto is such a simple sauce to make that you may never purchase a commercially prepared product again. An additional benefit of doing it yourself is that you can alter ingredients to suit your preferences — make it more garlicky, cheesy, or nutty. Use pine nuts in place of walnuts or sunflower seeds to make it more traditional. Make a lot of it in summer when fresh basil is abundant. Pesto freezes beautifully. — LA

1 In a food processor or blender, combine basil, Parmesan, oil, nuts, and garlic until smooth. Taste and adjust ingredients according to your preference.

2 Divide among freezer containers, adding a thin layer of oil to top of each container. Pesto will stay at optimal quality for up to 6 months in freezer or in an airtight container in refrigerator for up to 3 days.

INGREDIENTS

- 2 cups packed fresh basil leaves
- ¾ cup shredded Parmesan cheese (about 3 ounces)
- ¾ cup olive oil, plus more for freezing
- ½ cup walnuts or sunflower seeds
- 1½ teaspoons minced garlic

PACK IT UP

Four 4-ounce plastic containers, suitable for freezing

PLAY ON PESTO

MAKES 1⅓ cups

Basil may be the original star of pesto, but different greens offer their own spin. Spinach pesto is my favorite to toss with hot, cooked pasta, and arugula pesto is my preference to spread on a toasted baguette with goat cheese. Lemon juice gives it a nontraditional but bright touch. — LA

1 In a food processor or blender, combine spinach, cheese, oil, lemon juice, pecans, and garlic and blend until smooth. Taste and adjust ingredients according to your preference.

2 Divide among freezer containers, adding a thin layer of oil to top of each container. Pesto will stay at optimal quality for up to 6 months in freezer or in an airtight container in refrigerator for up to 3 days.

INGREDIENTS

- 2 cups packed fresh baby spinach or arugula
- ¾ cup grated Pecorino Romano cheese, or another similar hard, salty cheese (about 3 ounces)
- ¾ cup olive oil, plus more for freezing
- ¼ cup lemon juice
- ½ cup pecans
- 1 teaspoon minced garlic

PACK IT UP

Four 4-ounce plastic containers, suitable for freezing

RASPBERRY VINAIGRETTE

MAKES 1¾ cups

INGREDIENTS

- 1 cup olive oil
- ½ cup fresh or frozen raspberries, at room temperature
- ½ cup red wine vinegar
- 1 tablespoon balsamic vinegar
- 1 tablespoon honey
- 1 teaspoon spicy brown mustard
- ½ teaspoon salt
- ¼ teaspoon black pepper

This recipe was developed for those who would rather not use a commercially prepared product for the Berry-Roasted Chicken (page 56). And not to worry that this recipe doesn't quite make the 2 cups called for in that recipe — it will be plenty. You can use this vinaigrette any way you like, of course. I like it over a salad of robust greens such as arugula and dandelion, or subtle greens such as romaine and butter lettuce, garnished with crumbled blue cheese and toasted pecans. — LA

1 In a container with a tight-fitting lid, add the oil, raspberries, vinegars, honey, mustard, salt, and pepper. Shake vigorously.

2 Use immediately, or store in an airtight container in refrigerator for up to 1 week or in freezer for up to 3 months for optimal quality. Bring to room temperature before serving.

TERIYAKI SAUCE

MAKES 2 cups

This simple teriyaki-style sauce is just as tasty and convenient as anything you might buy in the store — but less expensive. Use it in our Teriyaki Chicken (page 55), or in other recipes, like the Rose City Teriyaki (page 96). — LA

1 In a small bowl, whisk together soy sauce, sugar, vinegar, oil, garlic, and ginger until sugar is dissolved.

2 Use immediately, or store in an airtight container in refrigerator for up to 1 week or in freezer for up to 3 months for optimal quality.

INGREDIENTS

- 1 cup soy sauce
- 1 cup firmly packed brown sugar
- ¼ cup red wine vinegar
- 1 tablespoon vegetable oil
- 2 teaspoons minced garlic
- 2 teaspoons minced ginger

BIG SAVINGS

Homemade teriyaki is easy to make and costs pennies on the dollar compared to the store-bought versions. Expect this to be a thinner consistency than bottled sauces on the market.

BREAKFAST,
SNACKS, AND SWEETS

BREAKFAST BURRITOS

MAKES 4 freezer meals, 5 servings each

INGREDIENTS

- 20 (10-inch) flour tortillas, uncooked preferred, such as Tortilla Land brand
- 1 dozen eggs, lightly beaten
- 3 pounds yellow-flesh potatoes, boiled and cut into bite-size pieces
- 1 cup sour cream
- 1 teaspoon salt
- 1 teaspoon black pepper
- 1 pound deli ham, cut into bite-size pieces
- 2 cups shredded cheddar cheese (about 8 ounces)

Enjoy a hot, nutritious breakfast that needs no preparation in the morning. Look for uncooked flour tortillas and cook them prior to assembly for a superior burrito. — LA

1 If you are using uncooked tortillas, cook them all according to package directions. Keep them warm in a clean, dry tea towel.

2 In a large greased skillet, scramble eggs over medium heat until just set.

3 In a large bowl, combine scrambled eggs, potatoes, sour cream, salt, and pepper. Stir in ham and cheese.

4 Lay all tortillas out on a work surface. Divide egg mixture evenly among tortillas (about ½ cup on each).

5 Wrap each tortilla burrito-style, then wrap each individually in foil or parchment paper then plastic wrap, depending on how you will reheat them. Divide evenly among freezer bags.

6 Seal and freeze. Food will stay at optimal quality for up to 2 months in freezer.

TO COOK ONE FREEZER MEAL

Thaw burritos in refrigerator or reheat them straight from freezer.

Microwave (parchment wrapped)

Remove plastic wrap, defrost, and reheat.

Oven (foil wrapped)

Bake in foil at 375°F (190°C) for 30 minutes if frozen, 300°F (150°C) for 30 minutes if thawed.

PACK IT UP

Aluminum foil or parchment paper and plastic wrap

Four 1-gallon freezer bags, labeled

CHEESE BISCUIT MIX

MAKES 8 freezer batches, 8 servings each

These biscuits have half the amount of butter of traditional biscuits, but you'd never know it by their rich flavor. Enjoy them with many of our entrées, especially the soups and chilis. — LA

INGREDIENTS

- 16 cups all-purpose flour
- 2 pounds sharp cheddar cheese, shredded
- ⅔ cup baking powder
- ¼ cup sugar
- 1 tablespoon salt
- 2 cups (4 sticks) butter, cut into 1-inch cubes

ON HAND FOR BAKING EACH BATCH

- ¾ cup milk

1 In a large bowl, combine flour, cheese, baking powder, sugar, and salt. Add butter; rub into flour until butter is in tiny pieces. Divide mixture evenly among freezer bags.

2 Seal and freeze. Food will stay at optimal quality for up to 6 months in freezer.

TO BAKE ONE BATCH

1 Completely thaw one batch in refrigerator.

2 Preheat oven to 425°F (220°C).

3 In a medium bowl, combine bagged mixture with milk, and stir to form a dough. Turn dough out onto a lightly floured work surface and knead until dough holds together. Pat into a circle 2 inches thick. Cut into 8 wedges.

4 Place wedges on an ungreased rimmed baking sheet. Bake for 15 to 20 minutes, or until golden brown.

PACK IT UP

Eight 1-gallon freezer bags, labeled

CHEESE BITES

MAKES 8 freezer packs, 12 bites each

At my house, I pull these versatile snacks out of the freezer to serve spur-of-the-moment visitors, to give dinner guests something to snack on before the meal is ready, as a make-ahead appetizer for the busy holiday season, or as a warm snack for the family on a cold afternoon. You can vary these snacks by adding a green olive or a nut to the center of each ball. — LA

1 In a large bowl, combine flour, cheese, butter, salt, and cayenne. Knead into a dough in the bowl. Roll dough into 1-inch balls and place on an ungreased rimmed baking sheet.

2 If using olives, form each ball around 1 olive. If using pecans, press 1 pecan half onto each ball.

3 Place cheese balls in freezer for 30 minutes.

4 Remove cheese balls from freezer. Place a dozen into each freezer bag.

5 Seal and freeze. Food will stay at optimal quality for up to 6 months in freezer.

TO BAKE ONE DOZEN CHEESE BITES

1 Thaw one bag in refrigerator or bake straight from freezer.

2 Preheat oven to 425°F (220°C).

3 Place cheese balls 3 inches apart on an ungreased baking sheet. Do not flatten. Bake 15 to 17 minutes if frozen, 13 to 15 minutes if thawed.

INGREDIENTS

- 5 cups all-purpose flour
- 2 pounds sharp cheddar cheese, shredded
- 2 cups (4 sticks) butter, softened
- 1 teaspoon salt
- ½ teaspoon cayenne pepper

  Small pimento-stuffed green olives, well drained (optional)

  Raw pecan halves (optional)

PACK IT UP

Eight 1-quart freezer bags, labeled

GOLDEN GRANOLA

MAKES 8 freezer meals, 3 cups each

My mom made granola from scratch when I was growing up, and to this day I cannot eat the boxed stuff from the store — it just doesn't compare! Here's my version of my mom's recipe. I keep this on hand, not just for my family to eat but also to give as birthday, housewarming, or hostess gifts. — LA

1 In a large bowl, mix oats, almonds, coconut, sesame seeds, sunflower seeds, wheat germ, cranberries, raisins, flour, and cinnamon.

2 In a medium saucepan, combine honey, oil, water, vanilla, and salt. Cook, stirring, over medium heat until sauce begins to boil. Remove from heat. Pour sauce over oat mixture and mix well.

3 Divide granola evenly among freezer bags.

4 Seal and freeze. Food will stay at optimal quality for up to 6 months in freezer.

TO BAKE ONE PACKAGE

1 Preheat oven to 275°F (135°C).

2 Spread frozen granola on an ungreased baking sheet. Bake, stirring every 10 minutes, for 30 minutes, or until golden brown.

3 Cool and store in an airtight container.

INGREDIENTS

- 12 cups old-fashioned rolled oats
- 2 cups almonds, chopped
- 2 cups unsweetened shredded coconut
- 2 cups untoasted sesame seeds
- 2 cups raw sunflower seeds
- 2 cups wheat germ
- 1 cup dried cranberries
- 1 cup raisins
- 1 cup whole-wheat flour
- 1 tablespoon ground cinnamon
- 2 cups honey
- 2 cups vegetable oil
- ⅔ cup water
- 2 tablespoons vanilla extract
- 2 teaspoons salt

PACK IT UP
Eight 1-quart freezer bags, labeled

NOT JUST FOR BREAKFAST

Although we most often eat granola in the morning with milk, it's also delicious eaten as a snack — sprinkle over yogurt or ice cream, or just eat by the handful!

PB&J BREAKFAST COOKIES

MAKES 4 freezer packs, about 8 cookies each

INGREDIENTS

- 1½ cups natural peanut butter
- 1 cup (2 sticks) butter
- 1 cup firmly packed brown sugar
- ½ cup apricot jam, preferably no sugar added
- ¼ cup molasses
- 4 eggs
- 2 teaspoons vanilla extract
- 4 cups old-fashioned rolled oats
- 3 cups whole-wheat flour
- 1 cup instant dry milk powder
- 1 cup sunflower seeds
- 2 teaspoons baking soda
- 1 teaspoon salt

PACK IT UP

Waxed paper

Four 1-gallon freezer bags, labeled

My friend Renée, who has a relatively large family, created a breakfast cookie recipe for those times when she needed something quick and nutritious for the morning meal. I have modified her recipe, but I kept her main goal in mind: to create a breakfast cookie that was both nutritious and tasty. — LA

1 Preheat oven to 350°F (180°C).

2 In a food processor, or stirring by hand in a large bowl, combine peanut butter, butter, sugar, jam, molasses, eggs, and vanilla. In a separate large bowl, mix oats, flour, dry milk, sunflower seeds, baking soda, and salt. Pour peanut butter mixture into oats mixture; combine well.

3 Scoop dough with a ¼-cup measure and place several inches apart on ungreased baking sheets. With your fingers or backside of a spoon, shape into 1-inch-thick patties. Bake for 13 to 16 minutes. Cool on baking sheets for 5 minutes, then transfer to a wire rack. Divide cooled cookies evenly among freezer bags, separating layers with waxed paper.

4 Seal and freeze. Food will stay at optimal quality for up to 6 months in freezer.

TO ENJOY

Remove desired number of cookies from freezer; thaw in refrigerator or at room temperature.

BAKE BEFORE FREEZING?

Unlike our sweet-cookie recipes, we like to bake these before freezing so they're easy to grab in the morning. The dough does freeze well, though, so if you prefer, freeze the dough as described in the cookie recipes beginning on page 227.

ZOO DAY SNACK MIX

MAKES 6 freezer snacks, I serving each

Like most children, my kids are nuts about the zoo and love pretending to be the animals they see there. This snack mix has all the right stuff: peanuts for your little elephants, banana chips for your little monkeys, mango for your little bats, and berries for your birds. Each ingredient helps reinforce the wonder and fun of acting like our creature friends. Add to the merriment by personalizing the snack bags to reflect the foods eaten by the animals at a zoo you frequent. Each snack bag holds enough for two children to share. — KN

1 Into each snack bag, place ½ cup animal crackers, ¼ cup banana chips, 2 tablespoons berries, 2 tablespoons mango, and 2 tablespoons peanuts. Seal bags and gently shake to combine ingredients; place snack bags in 1-gallon freezer bag.

2 Seal and freeze. Food will stay at optimal quality for up to 3 months in freezer.

TO ENJOY

Thaw desired number of snack bags in refrigerator.

INGREDIENTS

- 3 cups animal crackers (6 ounces)
- 1½ cups banana chips (6 ounces)
- 12 tablespoons dried berries or raisins (6 ounces)
- 12 tablespoons chopped dried mango (6 ounces)
- 12 tablespoons lightly salted peanuts (6 ounces)

PACK IT UP

Six snack or sandwich bags

One 1-gallon freezer bag, labeled

PUMPKIN MUFFINS

MAKES 4 freezer packs, about 9 muffins each

INGREDIENTS

- 3 cups all-purpose flour
- 3 cups whole-wheat flour
- 2 cups firmly packed brown sugar
- ⅓ cup dry milk powder (do not use instant)
- 2 tablespoons baking powder
- 1 tablespoon cake spice (such as Penzeys, or try our homemade version on page 131)
- 1 tablespoon ground cinnamon
- 1 teaspoon baking soda
- 1 (29-ounce) can pumpkin purée
- ½ cup (1 stick) butter, melted
- 6 eggs, beaten
- ⅔ cup milk
- 2 tablespoons double-strength vanilla extract

PACK IT UP

Four 1-gallon freezer bags, labeled

My children love anything with pumpkin. When developing this recipe, I was aiming for a delicious muffin with extra fiber and calcium for my kids. The vitamin A, whole-wheat flour, and added calcium make these muffins better than most commercial alternatives. — KN

1 In a large bowl, mix all-purpose flour, whole-wheat flour, sugar, dry milk powder, baking powder, cake spice, cinnamon, and baking soda.

2 In a separate large bowl, and using an electric mixer, mix pumpkin, melted butter, eggs, milk, and vanilla. Add half of pumpkin mixture to flour mixture, beating until just combined. Beat in remaining pumpkin mixture. Batter will be stiff.

3 Preheat oven to 375°F (190°C).

4 Grease three 12-cup regular muffin pans. (If you don't have enough muffin pans, bake muffins in batches.) Fill each cup two-thirds full with batter. Bake for 20 to 25 minutes, or until a knife inserted into center of a muffin comes out clean.

5 Allow muffins to cool until they are cool enough to handle, 3 to 5 minutes. Transfer muffins to a wire rack. Divide cooled muffins evenly among freezer bags.

6 Seal and freeze. Food will stay at optimal quality for up to 6 months in freezer.

TO ENJOY

1 Thaw desired number of muffins in refrigerator.

2 Reheat in microwave, in intervals of 10 to 15 seconds, until centers are warm.

DOUBLE VANILLA

You can find "double-fold" or "double-strength" pure vanilla at most grocery stores or from a variety of online retailers. If you can't find something to your liking, consider making your own vanilla extract. Add 2 or 3 vanilla beans to a quart of vodka, brandy, or rum; store in a cool, dark place, and you can begin curing your own extract.

CHERRY-ALMOND SCONE MIX

MAKES 5 freezer batches, 4–5 servings each

INGREDIENTS

9 cups all-purpose flour

1½ cups sugar

1 cup almonds, chopped fine (about 4½ ounces)

¼ cup baking powder

1 tablespoon salt

1¼ cups (2½ sticks) unsalted butter

2 cups dried cherries, chopped into ½-inch pieces (about 10 ounces)

ON HAND FOR COOKING EACH FREEZER BATCH

½ cup milk

½ cup sour cream

½ teaspoon almond extract

Flour, for kneading

Treat yourself with these scones and your favorite cup of coffee next weekend. — KN

1 In a large bowl, combine flour, sugar, almonds, baking powder, and salt. Add butter and rub into flour mixture until butter is in tiny pieces. Mix in cherries.

2 Divide mixture evenly among freezer bags, about 3 cups each. Freeze. Food will stay at optimal quality for up to 6 months in freezer.

TO BAKE ONE BATCH

1 Thaw one freezer bag of baking mix in refrigerator.

2 Preheat oven to 350°F (180°C).

3 In a large bowl, combine baking mix, milk, sour cream, and almond extract. Turn dough out onto a lightly floured work surface and knead until dough is slightly sticky to touch, adding more flour as needed. Pat into an 8-inch circle and cut into 8 wedges.

4 Place wedges on a lightly greased baking sheet. Bake for 18 to 20 minutes, or until scones are lightly browned.

TROPICAL FRUIT SMOOTHIES

MAKES 8 freezer batches, 1–2 servings each

Smoothies are great for a quick breakfast or a pick-me-up later in the day. Because the tropical fruit mix is naturally sweet, this recipe calls for plain yogurt. — LA

1 Divide fruit evenly among freezer bags. Into each bag, measure ½ cup yogurt and ¼ cup orange juice concentrate.

2 Seal and freeze. Food will stay at optimal quality for up to 2 months in freezer.

TO ENJOY
Thaw one bag in refrigerator just enough to remove mix from bag. Put smoothie in a blender and add 1 cup cold water. Blend until smooth.

INGREDIENTS

- 6 pounds frozen tropical fruit mix
- 1 (32-ounce) container plain yogurt
- 1 pint orange juice concentrate

PACK IT UP
Eight 1-quart freezer bags, labeled

STRAWBERRY SMOOTHIES

MAKES 8 freezer batches, 1–2 servings each

This recipe is designed so you can go from zero to smoothie in no time flat. Feel free to add fresh greens or your favorite protein powder before you whip it up. — LA

1 Divide strawberries evenly among freezer bags. Into each bag, measure ½ cup yogurt and ¼ cup orange juice concentrate.

2 Seal and freeze. Food will stay at optimal quality for up to 2 months in freezer.

TO ENJOY

Thaw one bag in refrigerator just enough to remove mix from bag. Put smoothie in a blender and add 1 cup cold water. Blend until smooth.

INGREDIENTS

- 6 pounds frozen strawberries
- 1 (32-ounce) container strawberry yogurt
- 1 pint orange juice concentrate

PACK IT UP

Eight 1-quart freezer bags, labeled

STAY COOL

If the smoothie thaws completely, simply blend with 1 cup ice.

BEACH DAY SNACK MIX

MAKES 6 freezer snacks, 1 serving each

INGREDIENTS

- 1½ cups dried banana chips (6 ounces)
- 12 tablespoons chopped dried mango (6 ounces)
- 12 tablespoons hulled sunflower seeds
- 12 tablespoons shredded coconut (3 ounces)
- 6 tablespoons white chocolate chips (such as Guittard)

Making healthful school lunches and after-school snacks can be a daily challenge. Kids, like adults, need variety in their diets even if they complain about it. I try to make this mix more appealing by using high-quality white chocolate chips. Kids enjoy this mix straight from the bag and as a topping for tropical ice-cream sundaes. — KN

1 Into each snack bag, place ¼ cup banana chips, 2 tablespoons mango, 2 tablespoons sunflower seeds, 2 tablespoons coconut, and 1 tablespoon white chocolate chips. Seal bags and gently shake to combine ingredients. Place all snack bags into 1-gallon freezer bag.

2 Seal and freeze. Food will stay at optimal quality for up to 3 months in freezer.

TO ENJOY

Remove desired number of snack bags from freezer; thaw in refrigerator.

PACK IT UP

Six snack or sandwich bags

One 1-gallon freezer bag, labeled

FIVE-SPICE COOKIES

MAKES 7 freezer packs, about 1 dozen cookies each

Here's another recipe I developed around a particular ingredient I wanted to try. These Asian-inspired treats offer a unique twist on a traditional butter cookie. — KN

1 In a large bowl, and using an electric mixer, cream sugar and butter. Beat in eggs, milk, and orange extract. In a separate large bowl, mix flour, baking powder, and salt. Add half the flour mixture to the butter mixture and beat well. Beat in remaining flour mixture.

2 To make topping: In a small bowl, mix sugar and five-spice powder.

3 Roll dough into 1-inch balls. Roll dough balls in topping and place on a rimmed baking sheet.

4 Place in freezer for 30 minutes. Remove dough balls from freezer and place a dozen into each freezer bag.

5 Seal and freeze. Food will stay at optimal quality for up to 6 months in freezer.

TO BAKE ONE DOZEN COOKIES

1 Preheat oven to 375°F (190°C).

2 Place frozen cookies 3 inches apart on a parchment paper–lined baking sheet.

3 Bake for 8 to 10 minutes, or until tops crack. Cool on baking sheet for 2 minutes, then transfer to a wire rack.

INGREDIENTS

- 3 cups sugar
- 2 cups (4 sticks) butter, softened
- 3 eggs
- ¼ cup milk
- 2 teaspoons orange extract
- 5½ cups all-purpose flour
- 2 tablespoons baking powder
- ½ teaspoon salt

TOPPING

- ½ cup sugar
- 2 teaspoons five-spice powder

ON HAND FOR BAKING

Parchment paper

PACK IT UP
Seven 1-quart freezer bags, labeled

OATMEAL COOKIES
WITH COCONUT AND MANGO

MAKES 6 freezer packs, about 1 dozen cookies each

I freeze cookie dough so I can bake fresh cookies at a moment's notice. This is a basic oatmeal cookie with a tropical twist. The dried coconut and mango make these cookies both crispy and chewy. — LA

1 In a large bowl, and using an electric mixer, cream butter, sugar, eggs, and vanilla. In a separate large bowl, mix flour, oats, coconut, mango, baking powder, baking soda, and salt. Add flour mixture to butter mixture and mix well.

2 Refrigerate dough for 1 hour, or until firm enough to handle.

3 Roll dough into 1-inch balls and place on a rimmed baking sheet. Place in freezer for 30 minutes.

4 Remove dough balls from freezer. Place a dozen into each freezer bag.

5 Seal and freeze. Food will stay at optimal quality for up to 6 months in freezer.

TO BAKE ONE DOZEN COOKIES

1 Completely thaw one bag in refrigerator.

2 Preheat oven to 350°F (180°C).

3 Place cookies 3 inches apart on a parchment paper–lined baking sheet. Flatten slightly with a fork. Bake for 14 to 16 minutes.

4 Cool on baking sheet for 2 minutes, then transfer to a wire rack.

INGREDIENTS

- 2 cups (4 sticks) butter
- 2 cups firmly packed brown sugar
- 2 eggs
- 2 teaspoons vanilla extract
- 3 cups all-purpose flour
- 3 cups old-fashioned rolled oats
- 1 cup unsweetened shredded coconut
- 1 cup chopped dried mango (8 ounces)
- 2 teaspoons baking powder
- 1 teaspoon baking soda
- 1 teaspoon salt

ON HAND FOR BAKING

Parchment paper

PACK IT UP
Six 1-quart freezer bags, labeled

PARCHMENT PAPER

We suggest parchment paper for our cookie recipes because it eliminates the need for greasing the baking sheet, which adds both a step and extra fat. The paper also makes moving the cookies a cinch — just lift the paper and transfer all the cookies to the wire rack in one move.

GINGER COOKIES

MAKES 5 freezer packs, about 1 dozen cookies each

INGREDIENTS

- 1½   cups (3 sticks) butter
- 1½   cups firmly packed brown sugar
- ½   cup molasses
- ¼   cup minced fresh ginger
- 2   eggs
- 4   cups all-purpose flour
- 1   tablespoon baking soda

These cookies are like gingersnaps, only without the snap — for the cookie lover who prefers soft, chewy cookies. Loaded with minced fresh ginger, this cookie is zingy and not too sweet. — LA

1 In a large bowl, and using an electric mixer, cream butter, sugar, molasses, ginger, and eggs. Add flour and baking soda, and mix well.

2 Refrigerate dough for 1 hour, or until firm enough to handle.

3 Roll dough into 1-inch balls and place on a rimmed baking sheet. Place in freezer for 30 minutes.

4 Remove dough balls from freezer. Place a dozen into each freezer bag.

5 Seal and freeze. Food will stay at optimal quality for up to 6 months in freezer.

TO BAKE ONE DOZEN COOKIES

1 Thaw one bag in refrigerator or bake straight from freezer.

2 Preheat oven to 350°F (180°C).

3 Place cookies 3 inches apart on an ungreased baking sheet. Do not use parchment paper here. Do not flatten dough balls. Bake for 15 to 17 minutes if frozen, 12 to 14 minutes if thawed.

4 Cool on baking sheet for 2 minutes, then transfer to a wire rack.

PACK IT UP

Five 1-quart freezer bags, labeled

THE COOKIE SCOOP

A handy tool to use for any kind of rolled or drop cookie, a cookie scoop lets you skip refrigerating the dough before handling. If you've never used one, you've never experienced how fast cookie making can be! Unlike other kitchen gadgets that end up cluttering the drawer, this one really gets used. Cookie scoops can be found at your local kitchen retailer.

VERY VANILLA
SNICKERDOODLES

MAKES 7 freezer packs, about I dozen cookies each

The secret to these cookies is high-quality fresh cinnamon. I buy cinnamon in smaller quantities, replacing old with new around Thanksgiving of each year, when I use it often in holiday baking. — KN

1 In a large bowl, and using an electric mixer, cream granulated sugar and butter. Beat in eggs, milk, and vanilla. In a separate large bowl, mix all-purpose flour, whole-wheat flour, baking powder, and salt. Add half of flour mixture to butter mixture, and beat well. Beat in remaining flour mixture. Batter will be stiff.

2 To make topping: In a small bowl, mix vanilla sugar and cinnamon.

3 Roll dough into 1-inch balls. Roll dough balls in topping and place on a rimmed baking sheet.

4 Place in freezer for 30 minutes.

5 Remove dough balls from freezer and place a dozen into each freezer bag.

6 Seal and freeze. Food will stay at optimal quality for up to 6 months in freezer.

TO BAKE ONE DOZEN COOKIES

1 Place frozen cookies 3 inches apart on a parchment paper–lined baking sheet.

2 Preheat oven to 375°F (190°C).

3 Bake for 8 to 10 minutes, or until tops crack. Cool on baking sheet for 2 minutes; transfer to a wire rack.

VANILLA SUGAR

Making your own vanilla sugar is easy and inexpensive: In the bowl of a food processor, put 1 cup granulated sugar and one-quarter of a vanilla bean. Process for 30 to 60 seconds. Remove any remaining large pieces of vanilla by hand or pour sugar through a strainer. Cure vanilla sugar in an airtight container at least 1 week before using.

INGREDIENTS

- 3 cups granulated sugar
- 2 cups (4 sticks) butter, softened
- 3 eggs
- ¼ cup milk
- 2 teaspoons double-strength vanilla extract (see box, page 220)
- 3½ cups all-purpose flour
- 2 cups whole-wheat flour
- 2 tablespoons baking powder
- ½ teaspoon salt

TOPPING

- Scant ½ cup vanilla sugar (see box below)
- 1 tablespoon ground cinnamon

ON HAND FOR BAKING

- *Parchment paper*

PACK IT UP
Seven 1-quart freezer bags, labeled

LEMON-LAVENDER
BUTTER COOKIES

MAKES 7 freezer packs, about 1 dozen cookies each

INGREDIENTS

2½   cups granulated sugar

2   cups (4 sticks) butter, softened

½   cup lavender sugar (see below)

3   eggs

¼   cup milk

2   teaspoons lemon extract

5½   cups all-purpose flour

2   tablespoons baking powder

½   teaspoon salt

TOPPING

½   cup lavender sugar

ON HAND FOR BAKING

Parchment paper

PACK IT UP

Seven 1-quart freezer bags, labeled

My family and I traveled to Sequim, Washington, one summer for its annual lavender festival. We toured several lavender farms, viewed acres of unique varietals, and enjoyed looking at the wares of local artists. I had fun observing the cornucopia of food and beverages made with fresh and dried lavender. My trip that day was the inspiration for these cookies. — KN

1 In a large bowl, and using an electric mixer, cream granulated sugar, butter, and lavender sugar. Beat in eggs, milk, and lemon extract. In a separate large bowl, mix flour, baking powder, and salt. Add half of flour mixture to butter mixture, and beat well. Beat in remaining flour mixture.

2 Roll dough into 1-inch balls. Pour topping into a small bowl. Roll dough balls in topping and place on a rimmed baking sheet.

3 Place in freezer for 30 minutes. Remove dough balls from freezer. Place a dozen balls into each freezer bag.

4 Seal and freeze. Food will stay at optimal quality for up to 6 months in freezer.

TO BAKE ONE DOZEN COOKIES

1 Preheat oven to 375°F (190°C).

2 Place frozen cookies 3 inches apart on a parchment paper–lined baking sheet.

3 Bake for 8 to 10 minutes, or until tops crack. Cool on baking sheet for 2 minutes, then transfer to a wire rack.

LAVENDER SUGAR

It's cheaper to make your own lavender sugar than to buy it. Into the bowl of a food processor, pour 1 cup granulated sugar and 1 teaspoon (edible) lavender flowers. Process for 30 seconds. Remove any remaining large pieces of lavender by hand or pour sugar through a strainer. Cure the sugar in an airtight container at least 1 week before using.

BRANCHING OUT

ADAPTING YOUR OWN RECIPES FOR MAKE-AHEAD MEALS

Once you've become experienced cooking with our method, there may come a time when you will want to adapt your own recipes for making ahead. Many of your favorite recipes will be good candidates for adaptation. Here are a few suggestions to consider.

CONSIDER THE MEAT. Look at the type and amount of meat in your original recipe. Divide the number of pounds in the value pack by the amount required in your recipe. For example, if the original recipe calls for 1½ pounds of pork tenderloin, take the package size of 4½ pounds and divide it by 1½, giving you the number 3. This tells you that you must multiply the recipe by 3 in order to use the entire package of pork. Begin with this general guideline, but expect to have to adjust individual recipe ingredients as discussed in the rest of this section.

ADJUST AMOUNTS FOR SALT AND PUNGENT SPICES. In our experience, many recipes call for too much salt in the first place. As a rule of thumb, when doubling or tripling a recipe, the scale needs to be increased by only half. For example, if the original recipe calls for 1 teaspoon of salt, use ½ teaspoon for each factor of multiplication of the recipe. So if you're doubling the recipe, you would use 1½ teaspoons of salt; for tripling, 2 teaspoons of salt total. Use this same rule of thumb for pungent spices, such as red pepper flakes, cinnamon, curry powder, cayenne pepper, and ground cumin. It's easier to add more seasoning to an underseasoned entrée than to diminish its effect after you've used too much.

BE CAREFUL WITH SALTY-FLAVORED SAUCES AND VINEGARS. Take care when multiplying the amounts of salty sauces such as soy sauce, Worcestershire sauce, ketchup, and flavored vinegars. If you want to keep the same amount of liquid, consider using reduced-salt versions of these products, or use broth, apple juice, or water as a substitute for a portion of the original amount (see Firehouse Pork Skewers on page 122 as an example). If the amount of liquid is not a concern, begin by cutting the original amount called for by one-third before multiplying the ingredient.

MULTIPLY MILD HERBS AND SEASONINGS NORMALLY. Amounts of mild herbs and seasonings can be successfully multiplied without adjustment. Basil, oregano, thyme, marjoram, garlic, and ginger are not as concentrated as other spices. It's still possible to use too much, but the probability that too much of these seasonings will ruin an entire batch of freezer meals is low.

TAKE NOTES AS YOU EXPERIMENT. Good record keeping will help you perfect a recipe you're adapting. Sometimes, the right amount of sauce, marinade, breading, or topping for one recipe will be too much or too little when multiplied for several recipes. Take notes while you're putting a recipe together, and after you've eaten the dish, too, so you'll know what to adjust the next time.

REMEMBER THAT CERTAIN INGREDIENTS, SUCH AS LETTUCE AND CUCUMBERS, DO NOT FREEZE SUCCESSFULLY. Other ingredients need special care before they go into the freezer. For example, raw potato will turn black in the freezer, so be sure to cook it first. Some vegetables freeze fine when raw as long as they're in a sauce or soup (carrots and celery, for example), but others should be blanched before freezing (cauliflower and green beans). See the box on page 13.

COMMUNITY COOKING OPTIONS

FOOD AS FELLOWSHIP

Many of the recipes in *Fix, Freeze, Feast* were developed while we were operating our own in-home meal-preparation businesses. Our businesses were a little different from a do-it-yourself group because we planned, shopped, and organized all the details for each group. Yet the recipes we developed lend themselves nicely to the small group that wishes to begin cooking together on its own. Cooking groups have been featured in many magazines and on popular websites because they're a great option for individuals who want to save time and money while enjoying the company of friends. What could be better? There are several ways to structure a do-it-yourself cooking group.

A COOKING CLUB. In a cooking club, the group agrees on what recipes to make, divides the shopping and organizing duties, and comes together on a specified day to prepare the meals *together*. This arrangement works well for members who have different skills and task preferences. For example, a person who dislikes shopping but doesn't mind dealing with money will probably be happy in a group with someone who loves shopping but dislikes money matters. It also works well for groups whose members don't want to go back home alone to cook in their own kitchens but have time for and are open to a more social experience of meeting new members and catching up with friends.

A COOKING CO-OP. In a co-op format, the group assigns recipes to individuals. Members make their freezer meals at their own homes and everyone meets later to swap meals. Each person is responsible for shopping and cooking all freezer meals of the assigned recipe. For example, in a cooking group of six, if Sue gets assigned Beef-Barley Soup and Jenny gets Sweet Asian Chicken, each will make six of their assigned recipe and then meet at a designated spot to swap. At the swap, each member gives five freezer meals away and receives five from the other members. The cooking co-op format works well for groups that have difficulty finding the time or space to gather for food preparation and cooking.

Whatever type of group cooking you choose — a club, a co-op, or a hybrid of the two — the benefits of cooking together remain the same. Together you share the costs, in time and money. Together you try new dishes without doing all the recipe research, planning, and work. And, perhaps most important, you get to do it all with friends, supporting one another, exploring new foods, and building relationships along the way.

FOOD AS SERVICE

Put your experience with make-ahead meals to good use for charity. The skills you've developed with this method could be used to make a wonderful donation to a nonprofit group. Schools, community service agencies, and religious organizations often need donations for auctions and other fund-raisers. A selection of frozen meals garners high bids — everyone wants make-ahead meals!

FOOD AS MINISTRY

When a friend or neighbor is facing a crisis or transition, a practical way to help is by providing a meal or two. People often offer their good intentions: "Let me know if there's anything I can do to help," but the person in crisis is then placed in the awkward position of having to ask for help. Even the most organized, accomplished cook may find it difficult to continue with regular tasks when faced with a major disruption in the regular routine. A hot meal is helpful, but frozen meals are more versatile. It can be a lifesaver to have a meal in the freezer several weeks after a life-changing event. If you show up with some frozen entrées in hand, you'll have the satisfaction of helping and your friend will appreciate your thoughtfulness.

Keeping meals on hand means needs can be met as they arise, not just when you have some extra time. Often meals are needed in a hurry, such as when there is a death, a sudden illness, or another unexpected trauma. Other times, the provision of meals can be planned for, as in the case of a scheduled surgery or a baby's birth or adoption. It won't take long before you begin to see needs all around you that can easily be met with make-ahead meals.

Structured ways of providing meals within communities exist, too. In many churches, support groups, and other groups of like-minded people, meal banks are becoming a popular way to keep nutritious food on hand for those in need. Small groups can gather to prepare freezer meals to be stored in a church or community freezer and delivered at the necessary time. The meal bank can be set up formally with set times for filling the freezer and specific people in charge of delivery, or it can be done more casually to supplement an existing hot meal delivery program.

Whether you want to explore this idea on your own or with a group, here are some things to keep in mind when considering recipe selection.

CHOOSE FOR FLAVOR. It's best to choose recipes that are middle-of-the-road on heat and spices. Children, the elderly, nursing mothers, people undergoing chemotherapy, and those who are ill may be more sensitive to spicy foods. This doesn't mean you have to eliminate recipes for such dishes from the menu; just leave out the red pepper flakes, cayenne pepper, or hot pepper sauce. Other good recipe choices are those that are classic family-friendly fare. Choose entrées that will have the widest appeal.

CHOOSE FOR EASE OF PREPARATION. You never know who might be preparing the entrée on the other end — perhaps a spouse or a teenager who has little experience in the kitchen. Make no assumptions about cooking abilities; select entrées that are easily baked or reheated. Unless you're certain a person has, say, a slow cooker, you will want to avoid recipes that require that method of cooking.

CHOOSE FOR VARIETY. When preparing freezer meals to hold as inventory, it's wise to have some selections for vegetarians, those with dairy allergies, and those who have fat, sugar, or salt restrictions. There's no need for a huge selection of items — just plan to have enough selections to meet the needs of a variety of potential recipients.

CHOOSE FOR COST. Maximize your budget by selecting recipes with less expensive cuts of meat and those that can be stretched by serving the dish over rice or noodles. Recipes that use meat in smaller proportions, such as for soup, chili, or meatballs, are also good choices.

CHOOSE FOR MORE THAN JUST DINNER. People appreciate receiving breakfast, lunch, and snack items just as much as dinner entrées.

PACKAGING

Always consider the needs of the recipient when you are packaging meals for others. It can be problematic for someone to keep track of containers that need to be returned. Unless you are certain that the recipient would prefer otherwise, package the meals in freezer bags, plastic containers, or foil pans, and let the recipient know that you don't expect to get them back.

Finally, if you've ever been the recipient of a meal when your life was turned upside down, you already know what a difference it can make. Until you have gone through an extremely stressful time yourself, providing a meal may seem like an insignificant way to help. But to the mom who has had a sleepless night with her new baby or to a family grieving the death of a loved one, a meal can be a lifeline. More than just nourishment for the body, it is one way to connect us as a community.

LABEL IT!

When you're giving away frozen meals, it's especially important to clearly label your packages with the name of the recipe, how many people it serves, and the directions for preparing it. Check out www.storey.com/freezer-labels for a pdf of recipe labels that you can download and print out.

QUICK **REFERENCE GUIDES**

COOK FROM FROZEN

Many recipes are equally successful when cooked from frozen. Thaw the food just enough to remove it from the container and place it in an oven-safe dish, a skillet, or a slow cooker according to directions. If you froze the food in glass bakeware, don't go from freezer to oven — extreme temperature changes can cause the dish to shatter.

If the meal is oven-baked, heat the oven to the temperature in the directions, and check food after 30 minutes to stir or separate as necessary for even baking. Increase baking time if needed. If the meal is in a skillet, begin to heat on low and increase temperature to the level recommended in the recipe instructions once the food has thawed. If the meal is in the slow cooker, count on cooking for the longer range of time.

Recipes that can successfully go from freezer to oven, stovetop, or slow cooker:

Chicken-Broccoli Bake, page 23

Chicken Curry, page 24

Mango-Cranberry Chicken, page 32

Swimming Rama, page 45

Honey-Glazed Chicken Thighs (always cook from frozen) , page 52

Royal Thai Thighs, page 54

Chicken à la King, page 62

Enchiladas Suiza Stack, page 66

Mulligatawny Soup, page 67

Chicken Wings, page 71

Beef and Bean Burritos, page 74

Cheesy Chilada Bake, page 75

Beef and Bow Tie Soup, page 77

Spanish Rice, page 78

Classic Lasagna, page 79

Sweet-and-Sour Meatballs, page 87

Mozzarella Meatballs, page 88

Salisbury Meatballs, page 89

Classic Chili, page 92

Beef-Barley Soup, page 104

Ginger Beef, page 105

Cheese Steaks, page 106

Cam's Ribs, page 119

Sticky Ribs, page 121

Pork Stew, page 128

Chile Verde, page 140

Garlic-Studded Pork Loin, page 136

Farmers' Market Soup, page 139

Rice Pilaf, page 147

Spanakopita, page 155

Roasted Sweet Potato and Black Bean Enchilada Stack, page 156

Manicotti, page 162

Vegetable Lasagna, page 163

Cream of Asparagus Soup, page 166

Garlic Mashed Potatoes, page 168

Baked Potato Chowder, page 169

Black Bean Soup, page 171

Black Bean and Vegetable Chili, page 172

Cream of Mushroom Soup, page 173

Tomato-Basil Soup, page 176

Breakfast Burritos, page 212

Cheese Bites, page 215

Golden Granola, page 217

Tropical Fruit Smoothies, page 223

Strawberry Smoothies, page 225

Five-Spice Cookies, page 227

Ginger Cookies, page 230

Very Vanilla Snicker-doodles, page 231

Lemon-Lavender Butter Cookies, page 232

Freezer Shelf Life

Frozen foods are safe to eat for much longer than the ingredients can maintain optimum flavor and texture. The freezing guidelines noted on each recipe and in the chart below are for highest quality.

2 MONTHS

Soups made with cream

Smoothies

Compound butters

3 MONTHS

Raw meats in sauce or marinade; meatballs

Lasagnas, stratas, and burritos

4 MONTHS

Soups

Uncooked whole chickens, roasts, and meatloaf

6 MONTHS

Baking mixes

Cookies and baked muffins

For information about freezing other food items, look online for the USDA-affiliated Cooperative Extension Service for resources.

FREEZER INVENTORY

Copy this page and use it to keep track of what is in your freezer and where it is located. Be sure to update it when you take meals out and place new ones in. Items are best used within 3 months of freezing unless otherwise noted in the recipe itself.

RECIPE	DATE MADE	NOTES	NUMBER OF MEALS

Metric Conversion Charts

Unless you have finely calibrated measuring equipment, conversions between US and metric measurements will be somewhat inexact. It's important to convert the measurements for all of the ingredients in a recipe to maintain the same proportions as the original.

Weight

TO CONVERT	TO	MULTIPLY
ounces	grams	ounces by 28.35
pounds	grams	pounds by 453.5
pounds	kilograms	pounds by 0.45

Volume

TO CONVERT	TO	MULTIPLY
teaspoons	milliliters	teaspoons by 4.93
tablespoons	milliliters	tablespoons by 14.79
cups	milliliters	cups by 236.59
cups	liters	cups by 0.24
pints	milliliters	pints by 473.18
pints	liters	pints by 0.473
quarts	milliliters	quarts by 946.36
quarts	liters	quarts by 0.946
gallons	liters	gallons by 3.785

ACKNOWLEDGMENTS

We are grateful to be surrounded by wonderful people, both professionally and personally, who have contributed to our project. Before this book ever made it to this incarnation, it had another life as a small self-published volume. Shawnee Halligan was an original contributor. Her sunny disposition and positive outlook made her a delight to work with. Some of her work is still reflected in this book.

Then, as now, we are privileged to work with many talented people who contribute their amazing skills and vision to this product behind the scenes through design, layout, editing, food photography, and printing. We appreciate the opportunity to work with Storey Publishing. We never knew the process could be so pleasant.

Thank you to our recipe testers. We are grateful that you were willing to undertake the task of trying new recipes, wading through our notes, and doing exactly as you were told!

We acknowledge the food enthusiasts, recipe writers, and culinary experts at large from whom we have gleaned ideas, tips, and much inspiration.

Loyal customers, old and new, we thank you for your enthusiasm and warm feedback. It has been uplifting.

Kati

Carl Jung once said, "The shoe that fits one person pinches another; there is no recipe for living that suits all cases." I am eternally grateful to my parents, children, family, and friends for their support while working on this book. Without you all, I would not have had the audacity and courage to create my own "recipe."

Lindsay

Cherished loved ones, my hope is that these three words are simply an echo of what you hear me say to you in person: You are treasured.

Kati, you are a reflection of strength and tenderness, wisdom and grace. I have loved working with you again.

And to the women and men who struggle to prepare meals and feel inadequate in your efforts: Be encouraged, my friends; you are much more competent and resourceful than you recognize.

INDEX

Page numbers in *italic* indicate photographs.

Dave's Swamp Blues Barbecued
Chicken, 28, 29

E

enchiladas
    Enchiladas Suiza Stack, 66
    Roasted Sweet Potato and Black
      Bean Enchilada Stack, 156

F

Fajitas, Beef, *98*, 99
Farmers' Market Soup, *5*, 139
"Feast Tonight" recipes
    Bourbon-Marinated Salmon, *194*,
      195
    Butternut Squash with Gorgonzola-
      Pecan Butter, 198
    Chicken Pizza with Port Barbecue
      Sauce, 39
    Chicken Salad with Port Barbecue
      Sauce, 38
    Cinco-Layer Bake, *58*, 59
    Dave's Barbecued Chicken Pizza, 30
    Dave's Skillet Hash, 29
    Fresh Vegetable Stir-Fry with Asian
      Marinated Tofu, 182, *183*
    Green Beans with Gorgonzola-
      Pecan Butter, 196, *197*
    Halibut with Chili-Lime Butter, 204,
      205
    Lemony Caesar Portobello
      Mushrooms, 185
    Linguine with Roasted Sweet Potato
      and Gorgonzola-Lemon Pepper
      Butter, 202
    Maple Portobello Mushrooms, *186*,
      187
    overview of, 2
    Portobello Mushrooms with Asian
      Market Marinade, 181
    Roasted Poblano-Potato Soup, 138
    Salmon with Walnut-Pesto Butter,
      199, *200*
    Sweet Chicken Tostada Crowns, 60
fellowship, food as, 235–236
feta cheese
    Feta and Spinach Lasagna Rolls,
      150, 151
    Spanakopita, *154*, 155
Firehouse Pork Skewers, 122, *123*
fish
    Bourbon-Marinated Salmon, *194*,
      195
    Halibut with Chili-Lime Butter, 204,
      205
    Salmon with Walnut-Pesto Butter,
      199, *200*
    Seafood Creole, 174, *175*
fish sauce, locating, 47
Five-Spice Cookies, 227, *228*
Flank Steak, 4Bs, 94

flavor, adjusting amounts of, 16–17
food safety, 12, 83
forgetting ingredients, 16
4 Bs Flank Steak, 94
4 Bs Grilled Chops, 110
freezer bags, 15, *15*, 17
freezer burn, 17
freezer space, conserving, 14
freezing
    baking before, 218
    best and worst foods for, 13, 235
    process overview, 12
French Onion Soup, 177, *178*
fresh foods, freezing of, 13
Fresh Vegetable Stir-Fry with Asian
    Marinated Tofu, 182, *183*
fried foods, freezing of, 13
Frittata, Asparagus and Potato, 146
Fruit Smoothies, Tropical, 223, *224*

G

garlic
    Garlic Mashed Potatoes, 168
    Garlic-Studded Pork Loin, 136, *137*,
      138
    overview of, 7
    Raging Garlic Pork Stir-Fry, 135
    Urban Garlic Chicken, 68
ginger
    Brown Sugar and Bourbon
      Marinade, 194
    Ginger Beef, 105
    Ginger Cookies, 230
    overview of, 7
glass, freezing and, 12
Gorgonzola cheese
    Butternut Squash with Gorgonzola-
      Pecan Butter, 198
    Gorgonzola-Lemon-Pepper Butter,
      201
    Gorgonzola-Pecan Butter, 196
    Green Beans with Gorgonzola-
      Pecan Butter, *197*
Gouda (Smoked) and Ham Strata,
    142, 143
Granola, Golden, *216*, 217
greasing, 7
Green Beans with Gorgonzola-Pecan
    Butter, 196, *197*

H

Habanero and Green Chile
    Hamburgers, 82
halibut
    Halibut with Chili-Lime Butter, 204,
      205
    Seafood Creole, 174, *175*
ham
    Breakfast Burritos, 212, *213*
    Chicken Cordon Bleu, 21

Smoked Gouda and Ham Strata,
    142, 143
Hamburgers, Habanero and Green
    Chile, 82
Hash, Dave's Skillet, 29
heat units, 54
honey
    Honey and Spice Pork Kabobs, 131
    Honey-Glazed Chicken Thighs, 52
    Sticky Drunk Pig on a Stick, 134

I

ice crystals, 14, 17
inventories, 15

J

jellies and jams
    Apple and Cranberry Pork Sirloin
      Roast, 126
    PB&J Breakfast Cookies, 218
    Pepper Jelly Pork Chops, 111
jerk seasoning
    Dave's Swamp Blues Barbecued
      Chicken, 28, 29, 30
    Uncle Dave and, 29

K

kabobs
    Honey and Spice Pork Kabobs, 131
    Peanut Satay, *50*, 51
ketchup, 88
kidney beans
    Black Bean and Vegetable Chili, 172
    Classic Chili, 92, *93*
kitchen preparation, 8

L

labeling, 10, 237
lasagna
    Classic Lasagna, 79, *80*, 81
    Feta and Spinach Lasagna Rolls, *150*,
      151
    Pork Ragout Lasagna, 132
Lavender-Lemon Butter Cookies, *233*
leaks, avoiding, 15
lemon juice
    from concentrate, 136
    fresh, 61
    Lemony Caesar Marinade, 184, 185
Lemon-Pepper Butter, Gorgonzola, 201
lemon(s)
    juicing, 61
    Lemon-Blueberry Strata, 152
    Lemon-Lavender Butter Cookies, *233*
lentils
    Farmers' Market Soup, *5*, 139
lime juice
    Chili-Lime Butter, 203
    Lime-Tequila Chicken, 48, *49*
lists, 6

Keep Dinner Simple
WITH MORE BOOKS FROM STOREY

by Andrea Chesman

Get a balanced dinner on the table in a single dish! These recipes include classic baked meals like chicken potpie and lasagna, as well as creative stovetop suppers like jambalaya and seafood paella, plus plenty of soups and hearty salads.

by Rachael Narins

Make your skillet sizzle! These 40 recipes show off the versatility of this affordable and timeless cooking method, from cast-iron classics like cornbread, pan pizza, and the perfect grilled cheese sandwich to future favorites like Korean fried chicken, skillet catfish, and s'mores.

by Maggie Stuckey

Bring the neighborhood together with your own soup night, choosing from 90 crowd-pleasing recipes for hearty chowders, chilis, and vegetable soups for any time of year. Additional recipes for salads, breads, and desserts round out the soup night experience.

Join the conversation. Share your experience with this book, learn more about Storey Publishing's authors, and read original essays and book excerpts at storey.com. Look for our books wherever quality books are sold or call 800-441-5700.